T0375610

"FOLLOW ME AS I FOLLOW CHRIST":

A DISCIPLESHIP CURRICULUM

DR. T. MARTIN FLOWERS

WestBow Press books may be ordered through booksellers or by contacting:

WestBow Press
A Division of Thomas Nelson & Zondervan
1663 Liberty Drive
Bloomington, IN 47403
www.westbowpress.com
844-714-3454

ISBN: 979-8-3850-2616-6 (sc)
ISBN: 979-8-3850-2617-3 (e)

Library of Congress Control Number: 2024910479

Print information available on the last page.

WestBow Press rev. date: 06/12/2024

TABLE OF CONTENTS

MODULE 1: THE CALL TO LEADERSHIP

MODULE 2: THE CHARACTER OF LEADERSHIP

Module 3: The Challenges of Leadership

Module 4: The Charges to Leadership

Workbook Exercises for Leader Reflection and Refreshing and Learner Responsibility

FOLLOW ME AS I FOLLOW CHRIST CURRICULUM OVERVIEW

INTRODUCTION

"Follow Me as I Follow Christ" (FMIFC) is a process that addresses two audiences: young men (learners) and faithful men (leaders). Throughout the process, the learners will develop and demonstrate skills and character traits modeled and taught by the faithful men who will entrust them with leadership responsibilities after successfully navigating the process. So, the young men must receive instruction, and the faithful men must be willing to share how their practical experiences align with the Word of God. Learners and leaders must be mature believers, convinced and convicted that God has called them to exercise their Spiritual leadership gift within the body of Christ. Paul listed the criteria for students and teachers in 1 Timothy 3:1-7.

CURRICULUM SCOPE

FMIFC focuses on a methodology church Leaders can utilize to prepare youths for leadership. FMIFC uses Paul's writings to Timothy to cultivate a learning environment of succession where mature leaders oversee the preparation of young leaders to take their place. From now on, "learners" will refer to the youth, and "leaders" will apply to the more mature overseers. The FMIFC development model has as its foundation two concerns Paul had regarding Timothy – being a youthful leader (1 Tim. 4:12) and his ability to groom generational successors given their relationship (2 Tim. 2:2). The leaders will be in a show, teach and tell mode while the learners will be in a listen, learn, and demonstrate mode.

Throughout the process, the emphasis will be on learning as the leader catechizes and models the desired outcomes, and the learner provides evidence of learning by participating in practical demonstrations of lessons learned in the various modules. Burke (2003) described the leader's responsibility as helping the learner view daily life experiences through the lens of the Gospel and Church teaching. In summary, Gresham (2006) considered the instructor to be a father figure gradually and progressively preparing the student to actively participate in the learning process as an essential element of their Spiritual formation. Execution of the FMIFC will require the youth to receive instruction, while the mature must be willing to share how their practical experiences align with God's Word.

Curriculum Rationale

Passing along lessons learned to the next generation of leaders is a historical and essential requirement in obedience to Jesus's directive to "make disciples" and to continue that activity "to the end of the age" (*English Standard Version*, 2001/2016, Matthew 28:19, 20). Repeatedly in Scripture, succession is the methodology employed to transition between Moses to Joshua, Elijah to Elisha, David to Solomon, and Jesus to His disciples. Our curriculum exemplar will be Paul to Timothy for the Ephesian church. Leaders, like David, serve the Lord's purposes in their generation (Acts 13:36), but there must be an ongoing proclamation to other generations (Ps. 71:18).

Churches can function without leadership but will operate below their capability level. Paul insisted that leaders provide order (Titus 1:5) but that the leaders must have demonstrated management capability to "care for God's church" (*ESV*, 2001/2016, 1 Timothy 3:5). There are many churches that do not have a succession plan nor are they making any preparations for the departure of their leadership. This curriculum will provide them with a tool for implementation.

Curriculum Timeline

The design for implementing this curriculum within a local church body is for two years. Discipling in preparation for leadership is a process that, as Bagby (2017) noted, requires some assembly to learn what is not known, unlearn that which requires elimination, and relearn forgotten means and measures. Jesus was with His disciples for three years, and Paul recounted in Galatians 1:18 a three-year learning period before meeting with the apostles in Jerusalem. FMIFC contains four modules – each requiring six months of learning, practicing, and reflecting. Learners may begin the process whenever their leader initiates it; however, the recommendation is for everyone involved to be together to have a standard beginning, experience, and goal.

Curriculum Objectives

1. For young learners to develop the confidence and competence required to lead a local church within two years.
2. For older leaders (instructors) to have a Pauline Development Guide to assess young learner development.
3. For leaders to have the courage and content to hold other leaders accountable.

Module 1

The Call to Leadership

MODULE INTRODUCTION

Hello! Welcome to "Follow Me as I Follow Christ" – FMIFC! FMIFC is a leadership development process for young leaders based on Paul's writings to Timothy. Our ultimate goals for this process are to minimize your anxieties about leadership at a young age and to prepare you to enable future leaders within your place of worship. The scheduled discipleship journey will take two years to complete, encompassing the Call, Character, Challenges, and Charges to Leadership. Each of you will have the opportunity to assess the certainty and direction of your calling, determine the fit of your character, understand the requirements, and prepare for the challenges of leadership somewhat peculiar to your age and experience.

Module One Overview

	Lesson One: Foundations of Establishing Discipling Relationship	**Lesson Two:** Determining the Certainty of Calling	**Lesson Three:** Identifying the Category of Calling
Overview:	* Desire to lead is imperative. * Emphasis will be on teaching for the leaders and on learning for the learners. * Leaders must lead by modeling.	* The call to leadership is only for some. * Confidence in proceeding increases with confirmed conformity to God's Word.	* The superhighway of leadership has numerous offramps. * Square pegs do not fit in round holes.
Objectives:	* To establish the authoritative source of calling. * To make calling and election sure. * To model godly character. * To understand, initiate, and implement succession.	* To determine suitability for leadership. * To share God's call on the leader's life for leadership.	* To describe and assess areas of giftedness. * To suggest avenues of service in leadership.
Scripture Readings:	1 Timothy 1:1, 12-14, 2:7,4:14, 5:22, 2 Timothy 1:1, 6, 8-14, 2:2, 3:10-17	1 Timothy 1:1, 6-7, 2:7, 2 Timothy 1:1, 5-6, 11	1 Timothy 2:7, 3:1, 8, 2 Timothy 1:6, 11
Vocabulary/Key Words:	Service, teacher, overseer, calling, reproof, correction, training in righteousness	Command, apostle, appointed	Deacon, gift, good work

MODULE ONE – LESSON ONE

FOUNDATIONS OF ESTABLISHING DISCIPLING RELATIONSHIPS

Overview

- The desire to lead is imperative.
- Emphasis will be on teaching for the leaders and learning for the learners.
- Leaders must lead by modeling.

Lesson Objectives

- To establish the authoritative source of calling.
- To make calling and election sure.
- To model godly character.
- To understand, initiate, and implement succession.

Scripture Readings

- 1 Timothy 1:1, 12-14, 2:7, 3:1, 4:14, 5:22
- 2 Timothy 1:1, 6, 8-14, 2:2, 3:10-17

KEY WORDS

Service
Overseer
Reproof
Training in Righteousness
Teacher
Calling
Correction

OVERVIEW

DESIRE TO LEAD

Your presence indicates your desire to lead, and learning about leadership in the body of Christ is paramount to your effectiveness. Paul told Timothy that desiring to lead God's people was noble and commendable (1 Timothy 3:1). The desire is good. As Willis (1994) posited, there were characteristics required of a candidate before advancing them in the process of taking on a position of authority. Like any other entity, churches need leadership to operate effectively and orderly. When Engstrom (1978) evaluated church leaders, he noted that there was a scarcity of people in the church who would step up and take on significant leadership roles – not a shortage of people but people willing to do what is necessary to lead effectively. By stepping forward, you have taken the first step to be an example to the believers.

EMPHASIS ON TEACHING AND LEARNING

Think of this process in terms of becoming a disciple. When Jesus spoke to those Luke described as His followers, Jesus provided them with the terms to which they would have to voluntarily subscribe if they were going to be His disciples or choose to only travel with Him. Dowd (2015) highlighted the personal difficult decisions required if Jesus's followers were to continue following Him and advance their relationship to the next level. The three conditions Jesus outlined for them in Luke 9:23 included denying themselves, taking up their crosses daily, and then following Him. Jesus called His disciples to follow Him, and now He is telling them they must make some character changes by denying themselves; they have a requirement charge to keep – taking up their cross, and they would agree to accept the challenges of following Him and being an active participant in His earthly mission. You are all here voluntarily, and we offer you this opportunity to "Follow Me as I Follow Christ."

The Necessity of Leadership Modeling

There will be leaders and learners as you work through the process. The leaders will reflect on their walk with Christ as they guide and assess the learners. Our process derives its name from 1 Corinthians 11:1, requiring the leaders to maintain the necessary level of spirituality of those leading a local church body. James warned those considering the role of being a teacher, and MacGorman (1986) supplemented the warning by noting that whatever prestige and privilege they may derive from instructing must be balanced against the "commensurate vulnerability to divine disfavor" (p. 31). There is a seriousness associated with leading that leaders cannot overlook and that learners must develop an awareness of. Willis (1994) cautioned leaders against authoritarian oversight and suggested leadership characterized by persuasive teaching of the leaders and viewing their lifestyle. Jesus's disciples heard His teachings and witnessed His daily interactions with people for three years. In keeping with Paul's directive to Timothy "not to be hasty in the laying on of hands" (*ESV*, 2001/2016, 1 Timothy 5:22), the FMIFC process has a scheduled two-year duration. This timeframe will allow learners to absorb instruction and observe lifestyle as the interactions in varying circumstances occur.

OBJECTIVES: LESSON ONE

ESTABLISH THE SOURCE OF CALLING

So, you want to be a leader of God's people? Paul told Timothy, "If anyone aspires to the office of overseer, he desires a noble task" (ESV, 2001/2016, 1 Timothy 3:1). What is interesting, as Thomas and Köstenberger (2017) pointed out, is that Paul does not mention a divine calling for the person - it is that person's aspiration which initiates the movement towards leadership. MacDonald (1990) conjectured that the Holy Spirit is the source of inspiration to seek this position of authority and responsibility. The desire to serve here indicates men who have set a lofty goal for themselves that will require them "to give an account" for those they lead (*ESV*, 2001/2016, Hebrews 13:17). Their desire is not a casual, carefree one but is one for which they are willing to stretch themselves to achieve the desired endstate fully.

After the person has expressed a desire for leadership, godly men should be able to recognize the quality of the ambitious person and agree with their intentions, disagree, or determine the developmental way forward. Luke recorded the high commendations of the Brothers, who were familiar with Timothy, and Paul agreed with their assessment, deciding to have Timothy accompany him on mission trips (Acts 16:2). As an outward demonstration of their concurrence with Timothy's Holy Spirit guided enthusiasm and their approval, a group of elders (1 Timothy 4:14) and Paul (2 Timothy 1:6) laid hands on Timothy. When the elders and Paul publicly placed their hands on Timothy, they did not impart a gift to him; they agreed with what the Holy Spirit had already done in his life (MacDonald, 1990). They recognized Timothy's desire, encouraged his development, and informed the body of believers of their confidence in what God was growing in Timothy.

Now, you have an opportunity for reflection. Your participation signals your aspiration, so how has the Holy Spirit led you to believe your calling to lead God's people? Timothy accepted Paul's invitation to travel with him, and Scripture does not record Timothy offering any pushback to Paul's suggestion to lead the Ephesian church. Buying into Paul's direction would require Timothy not to have an agenda because servants do not have agendas. The master's agenda is the servant's agenda. MacDonald (1990) clarified the difference between a servant and a friend using John 15:15 by noting that servants only do the work marked out for them without knowing how the finished product will look or function.

Conversely, friends have the confidence of the master builder and familiarity with the plans, process, and product. Paul knew the situation and realized the primary step was to be a servant of all the Ephesians. As Jesus instructed, the greatest must be a servant. The first must be a slave of all (Mark 10:44). As the leader, Timothy would be on display, modeling for the church the behaviors they should emulate (1 Timothy 3:15; 4:12). The only way to get better at an activity is the repetitive practice of that activity in varying environments comparable to the locus of praxis.

As you reflect on your decision to step into leadership, you will have to have the personal assurance that this is where the Holy Spirit is leading you and that you are taking these steps willingly and not under compulsion. You must understand that your leadership is akin to your ability and desire to submit to oversight. As Peter encouraged the believers to confirm their calling and election, Marzahn (2021) reasoned that assured conviction will carry you as a leader through difficult circumstances when others may challenge your call. If you do not have the courage and confidence that comes with conviction, you are more likely to change course – possibly leaving the path marked out for you by the Holy Spirit.

MAKE THE CALLING SURE

In our next lesson, we will cover the importance of your conviction of calling, but now we want you to know how Paul expressed certainty about his role in Timothy's life. We will focus on the verses indicating the source of Paul's calling and authority to disciple Timothy – 1 Timothy 1:1, 12-14, 2:7, 2 Timothy 1:1, 11.

1 Timothy 1:1

Paul is writing a letter to Timothy – a person, Timothy, and not a body of people- and he wants to drive home specific points about who he is and why it matters who he is to Timothy. He begins this letter by identifying himself, stating his role, and the source of his authority. Thomas and Köstenberger (2017) homed in on Paul's description of his appointment being "by command of God" so that he could emphasize that Timothy was also under orders. Although God's demands compelled and commanded their obedience, there was no coercion. So, Paul acknowledged his appointment as a command requiring complete compliance. As MacDonald (1990) pointed out, doing God's work God's way was not a means of livelihood, nor was it of man's design. Paul was writing with God as his source of authorization to communicate the truths of God in demonstrations of power.

1 Timothy 1:12-14

Here, Paul reminded Timothy of who he was before his encounter with God, how and why God changed him, and who he was due to his conversion. Whenever Paul told the story of his transformation, he highlighted how vehemently he opposed those he now belonged to. God in Paul's life was "an intrusive force" who reshaped his perspective and altered his circumstances with inexplicable mercy (Brueggemann, 1992, p. 741). Paul's conversion provided tangible evidence of God's direct involvement in his situation. In these verses, Paul again emphasizes that God, not man, was the source of his appointment. What we can see here is that God calls whom He will and uses them as He determines (Proverbs 16:4). For the leader and the learner, the past is in the past because when God chooses a person, He makes them into new creations (2 Corinthians 5:17) with a mission to forget the past and press on to obtain the prize (Philippians 3:13). Paul wanted Timothy to understand that God commissioned him to perform a special mission – to point him in the way that he should go to lead the Ephesian church.

1 Timothy 2:7

Many teachers in Ephesus proclaimed their teachings as truth, so Paul went to lengths to distinguish himself from those purveyors of false teachings. His primary vehicle of separation was that he was serving in a God-appointed ministry as a preacher, an apostle, and a teacher. Paul specifies each of these roles for Timothy to take note of when Paul was performing in each position. MacDonald (1990) clarified the functions like this – preachers proclaim the gospel; apostles are church planters who speak with direct authority from Jesus Christ, and teachers understandably explain the Word of God. The teachers Paul was sending Timothy to refute were false teachers who were independently attempting to replace God's authority by taking on roles for which God had not appointed them and alleging authority God had not granted them. Timothy witnessed Paul's efficacy in his God-appointed roles as he traveled with Paul. He heard Paul credit his abilities and accomplishments to the power he utilized through the Holy Spirit (Lim, 1987). Paul's speaking style and use of words may have been like the false teachers, but the power of God working through him was evident and distinguished him from the false teachers.

2 Timothy 1:1

Paul is writing a different letter to his son in the faith, and in doing so, he re-establishes who he is and by what authority he writes. At the time of this writing, though, Paul is awaiting death and softens his words to Timothy, ascribing his appointment to the will of God versus the command of God (Thomas & Köstenberger, 2017). Thomas and Köstenberger (2017) continued with Paul establishing a familial relationship with Timothy, his primary disciple, describing him in a role warranting taking exhortations and instructions. While Paul's tone seems softened, the message he continues to communicate to Timothy is that he is writing under the authority of God, from whom he accepted his responsibilities and who is fully obeying. This is a different letter, but it has the same authoritative source as the previous writing and the same author Timothy has seen demonstrating the power of God.

2 Timothy 1:11

Once again, Paul resorts to redundancy for emphasis. God has given him the responsibility and authority to be a preacher, apostle, and teacher. Evans and Holman (2019) described the significance of these Christ-appointed responsibilities: the preacher was to proclaim the good news; the apostle served as a leader and messenger with God-ordained authority; and the teacher provided instruction from the Word. Timothy's familiarity with Paul and his manner of life crystallized how he should respond to Paul's instructions in this letter. From Paul's letter to the church at Thessalonica and because he recognized the authority accompanying preachers, apostles, and teachers, Timothy respected the authenticity and accuracy of Paul's instruction (1 Thessalonians 5:12). The repeated reminders all reinforced Timothy's understanding that the source of authority Paul had for writing the letters to him came directly from God and required complete obedience.

Model Godly Characteristics

The ultimate goal of this process is for the leaders to model for the learners how to comport themselves – "Follow Me as I Follow Christ." When Paul and Silas visited Lystra, Paul became acquainted with Timothy and had him accompany them as they conducted mission trips. Following their journeys, Timothy partnered with Paul in Berea, Athens, Macedonia, Greece, Corinth, Philippi, Colossae, Rome, Thessalonica, and Ephesus. Timothy had been with Paul when Paul revealed to those traveling with him that the Holy Spirit made it clear to him that every city he visited would either put him in prison or assault him physically and mentally (Acts 20:23). Yet Timothy witnessed that Paul continued ministering from city to city. Because Timothy was a student of the Word, he understood from James's writing that trying a person's faith produces commitment that would enable the tested person to mature in their relationship with God (James 1:3-4).

When my Mom used to make her clothing, she would use patterns that she would overlay on the cloth she used. The pattern served as a guide for assembling the dress. In the same way, MacDonald (1990) described Paul's pattern for life as an overlay for Timothy to utilize in ministry. Timothy saw Paul's love for God, for God's people, and for those who would perish without God. By demonstrating his love relations before Timothy, Paul modeled how to be rightly related vertically and horizontally (Evans & Holman, 2019). A leader discipling a learner must visibly model examples of Christ and stay in step with the Holy Spirit (Galatians 5:25). Paul's godly lifestyle in words, deeds, and power should be the example for Timothy to follow.

UNDERSTAND THE ROLE OF SUCCESSION

Paul wanted to instill a final godly characteristic in Timothy: doing what is needed to prepare the next generation of godly leaders. MacDonald (1990) posited that Paul understood the importance of transmitting truth from generation to generation and inferred from Paul's admonition in 2 Timothy 2:2 the passing of the torch to four generations of believers. What Timothy would be passing, though, would be what he had heard and seen Paul say and do. Paul wanted Timothy to grasp the importance and necessity of ensuring "a succession of competent teachers" (MacDonald, 1990, p. 930). It was not enough to start the work in Ephesus – Paul wanted to complete the job or make provisions for its completion.

For work to continue, entities and individuals benefit from developing succession plans that prepare the organization to have continuity of leadership. Rothwell (2010) highlighted continuity in critical positions, organizational knowledge, and vision. In summarizing the work of the organizational initiator or leader, Schein (2010) posited that developing beliefs, values, and rules were essential to establishing the organization they would eventually pass on to the successor. Paul was the initiator of the Ephesian church, and he passed on valuable lessons to his "true child in the faith" (*ESV*, 2001/2016, 1 Timothy 1:2). Learning those lessons would prepare Timothy to assume leadership of the church in Ephesus (MacDonald, 1990). As relationships between the organization and the successor mature, Rothwell (2010) specified that the Ephesian church would benefit by having the right talent to meet future needs as they emerge. Timothy had traveled on mission trips with Paul, so he was very familiar with Paul's leadership methodology and manner of life.

So, what is succession? Rothwell (2010) labeled succession in terms of a planning management program as "a deliberate and systematic effort by an organization to ensure leadership continuity in key positions, retain and develop intellectual and knowledge capital for the future, and encourage individual advancement" (p. 6). Gray (2014) scoped the definition by specifying that the process identifies and develops vital organizational leaders. While much discussion centers around leadership positions, Rothwell (2010) broadened the discussion to include key positions regardless of category. The FMIFC process will explore the elements in Paul's transitional preparation for Timothy to accept his successional role in the Ephesian Church.

MODULE ONE - LESSON TWO

DETERMINING THE CERTAINTY OF CALLING

Overview

- The call to leadership is only for some.
- Confidence in proceeding increases with confirmed conformity to God's Word.

Lesson Objectives

- To determine suitability for leadership.
- To share God's call on the leader's life for leadership.

Scripture Readings

- 1 Timothy 1:1, 6-7, 2:7
- 2 Timothy 1:1, 5-6, 11

Key Words

Command
Apostle
Appointed

OVERVIEW

Limited Call to Leadership

At one time, the tagline for the United States Marine Corps stated that they were looking for "A few good men." In that regard, God is always looking for the right number of people to act in such a way that He gets the glory. When Gideon faced the Midianites, who were so numerous that they "could not be counted" (*ESV*, 2001/2016, Judges 6:5), God decreased Gideon's forces so that they would not believe their might caused them to triumph. MacDonald (1990) posited an unintentional tribute to Paul and Silas when the Thessalonians said of them that they had "turned the world upside down" (*ESV*, 2001/2016, Acts 17:6). When acting as almighty God's chosen instruments, there is not a need for excessive numbers. God proclaimed that the outstanding accomplishments of His people are not a result of might or power but because of His Spirit's involvement (Zechariah 4:6). Your effectiveness as a godly leader will not come because of your magnetic personality or your highly developed intelligence. Your competence and sufficiency will reflect your submission to the work of the Holy Spirit in your life.

There have been many who have started the leadership journey, but only a tiny percentage of them have reached their destination. Some have fallen along the wayside because their motivations were misaligned, and others have had insufficient, inaccurate, or inconsistent ideas about the responsibilities associated with leadership. Scripture is replete with how

God protects His glory by separating the contenders from the pretenders. We already mentioned Gideon's experience. Other instances include the narrow gate leading to life (Matthew 7:14); many called, but only a few were chosen (Matthew 22:14); and not many should become teachers (James 3:1). As a Timothy, you may have to interact with those who have no understanding about the ideas "about which they make confident assertions" (*ESV*, 2001/2016, 1 Timothy 1:7). This work is not for everyone. When the cares of the world and people's burdens begin to weigh on the pretenders, they fade away because they are operating using their might and power and have not availed themselves of the Holy Spirit.

Confidence Confirmed by Conformity

Paul saw within Timothy leadership qualities needing exercise by use because he had heard great things about him, and he had spent time with him observing his manner of life. Because Timothy had leadership potential bottled up inside of him, he needed to allow what God placed in him and that the elders noted when they laid hands on him (1 Timothy 4:4) and what Paul confirmed by also laying hands on him (2 Timothy 1:6) to work its way out. So, as Paul wrote to Timothy, Paskah et al. (2022) pointed out that Paul was eager to confirm Timothy's education, confirm his knowledge of Paul's way of life, and confirm Timothy's commitment to Spiritual growth and development. We hope you will develop confidence by demonstrating these three elements at this stage. Paul, convinced of God's call on his life, challenges learners to take in the words of the leaders as they observe their/our conformity to the teachings.

OBJECTIVES: LESSON TWO

DETERMINE THE SUITABILITY FOR LEADERSHIP

Whenever employers consider applicants for a position, one of their first points of examination is the applicants' qualifications relative to the position requirements. A wise applicant will conduct a similar exam before applying for the position. We have already noted Paul's commendatory statement about the goodness of a person aspiring to the "task" of leadership (*ESV*, 2001/2016, 1 Timothy 3:1); however, desiring a position differs from doing the required tasks to qualify one to be appropriate for employment. Paul's certainty of Timothy's leadership qualities sprang from his knowledge of Timothy's reputation (Acts 16:1-3), his godly heritage (2 Timothy 1:5), and his potential for developing his giftedness (2 Timothy 1:6). While you may or may not come from a God loving family, having a good reputation and giftedness are of primary importance. Let us examine further Timothy's case for suitability.

Good Reputation

While Jesus did not do deeds to establish a reputation, He had one, nonetheless. Luke summarized a common perception of Jesus when he stated, "He went about doing good and healing all who the devil oppressed" (*ESV*, 2001/2016, Acts 10:38). Earlier, we spoke of Paul and Silas, whose reputation was that they had turned the world upside down. When Paul visited Lystra, he met a disciple, Timothy, whom the people thought very highly of. Upon confirmation of Timothy's reputation, Paul wanted him to travel with him. Barry et al. (2012) described one's reputation as the estimation received from God or other people and emphasized the importance of having a positive reputation with those outside Christianity. Timothy's reputation began in his home community and spread due to his association with Paul. Each time Scripture refers to Timothy, with one exception being Hebrews 13:23, it is because of his relationship with Paul (Hull, 1959). Relationships are essential to understand that you become like those you hang around. As Paul declared in 1 Corinthians 15:33, "Bad company ruins good morals." Your company influences who you become and how others view you.

After taking Timothy onboard, he was with Paul in his travels. Hull (1959) noted John Mark, Timothy, and others who accompanied the primary messengers learning while assisting. Timothy's service prompted Paul to build up Timothy's credibility by describing him as a fellow worker (Romans 16:21), his beloved and faithful child (1 Corinthians 4:17), and as a servant of Christ Jesus (Philippians 1:1). Paul heard of Timothy's way of life, walked with Timothy alongside him, and concluded Timoth's "proven worth" was the reason for Paul partnering with him in spreading the gospel.

You should not underestimate the value of having a positive standing with God's people. However, your reputation before the world is of great importance. As Merkle (2014) posited, having an unstained reputation with those outside the body of Christ is a non-negotiable quality for determining suitability for leadership. Leaders and learners should primarily be concerned about the 'You can't judge me' attitude of young folks today. People can and will judge you, but as Peter encouraged, your reputation should be so sterling that when false accusations arise, those who make them will be ashamed for proposing such preposterous judgments (1 Peter 3:18). Allow Jesus's command to guide your reputation making – "Let your light shine before others, so that they may see your good works and give glory to your Father in heaven" (*ESV*, 2001/2016, Matthew 5:16). Periodically, we all need to do a light check to determine if our works are pointing people to God or are we seeking glory for ourselves. Your reputation will be what you allow it to be.

Godly Heritage

How often has someone mentioned that you remind them of one of your relatives? You may have also made that observation about someone else. Paul was familiar with Timothy's family, and some have conjectured that Paul was the recipient of hospitality extended to him by Timothy's mother and grandmother (Hull, 1959). When Paul wrote Timothy, he reminded Timothy of his godly heritage of faith passed from his grandmother, Lois, to his mother, Eunice (2 Timothy 1:5). Evans and Holman (2019) posited the importance of passing the faith from one generation to the next to preserve the culture and noted the godly influence the female family members had on Timothy. There is no positive proof of Timothy's Greek dad converting to faith in Jesus Christ, but his mother and grandmother passed on the truths of Christianity to Timothy (MacDonald, 1990). The influence of Timothy's mother and grandmother likely catalyzed his conversion when Paul first visited Lystra (Hull, 1959).

Not only did Timothy have a righteous mom and grandmother, but Paul claimed him to be his Spiritual offspring. Hull (1959) connected the five times Paul referred to Timothy as his beloved or legitimate Spiritual child with their intimate father-son relationship that met a need for both. Paul never had a physical son, and Jewish people considered Timothy to be an illegitimate child because his father was Greek and his mother was Jewish (Hull, 1959). Spiritually, Timothy's line came through his grandmother, his mother, and Paul, so Evans and Holman (2019) pointed out the significance of godly heritage to a family. By entrusting the Ephesian church into Timothy's care, Paul was, in essence, passing along an inheritance to Timothy – his Spiritual child who benefitted from his teaching.

One may benefit from a godly heritage; however, a godly legacy is not a prerequisite or a non-negotiable quality for Spiritual leadership. Israel and Judah's kings were good and evil and had offspring who succeeded them that were both good and bad. God's words recorded by Ezekiel declared that each person was responsible for their righteous or wicked deeds and that the sons were not accountable for the fathers or the fathers for the sons (Ezekiel 18:20). So, each person who aspires to leadership must decide how they will live their life. We will cover this in more detail later. Still, Paul challenged Timothy to act like him by passing on the things he learned to faithful people who would be able to pass the knowledge on to others (2 Timothy 2:2). The torch passing Paul challenged Timothy to do encompassed three generations – like grandmother to mother to son. Whether it is your physical or Spiritual child, God challenges you to develop your godly heritage by passing along the wisdom you gained to others. God is saying that the disciple must become a discipler. The process in which you are involved will require you as a learner to be a leader who prepares other learners through instruction and lifestyle, giving them a model to extend or begin their godly heritage.

Gift for Development

Timothy developed and had his reputation and godly heritage externally set – qualities for which he had minimal involvement. While others influenced young Timothy's life, Paul was eager to see the spark of Timothy's giftedness grow into a flame (2 Timothy 1:6). His desire was for Timothy to work out what was in him, and Paul knew it was in him because Paul was a part of the council of elders who laid hands on him (1Timothy 4:14; 2 Timothy 1:6). Based on Paul's encouragement in 1 Timothy 1:7, Kleinig (2017) proposed that Paul's words to Timothy during the ordination may have been a prayer the God would inject Timothy with the gifts of power, love, and a sound mind. McKenzie (2006) offered that though these gifts may have been resident within Timothy, they were contingent on him awakening them, rekindling them by allowing the Holy Spirit to have complete control of their exercise.

As you work your way through this discipleship experience, your giftedness will come to light, as well as your areas for strengthening. Timothy was shy and not very outspoken. Lawson (2002) provided the backdrop for why Timothy had to awaken and rekindle what was in him. Timothy was a young man going into a church that had not requested his presence and likely had several wealthy congregants prepared to pounce on Timid Timothy (Lawson, 2002). Timothy had to get over himself and those physical and mental limitations that might cause him to shrink back from carrying out God's call for his life. You will also have to get over yourself. Evans and Holman (2019) clarified that if Timothy had not fully exercised his giftedness, it would have been detrimental to the believers in Ephesus. MacDonald (1990) recognized power, love, and a sound mind as gifts Timothy was to use to "serve valiantly, endure patiently, suffer triumphantly…and die gloriously" (p. 926). Leadership is a requirement and a responsibility mandating commitment to the cause of Christ above all that humanly restricts our capacity to serve. While God's love constrains us to lead in a godly manner, our concern for others also must move us to the next level of effective leadership.

When Michael Jordan was in High School, the first year he tried out for the team, he was unsuccessful. His lack of success and commitment to succeed drove him to work persistently on improving his skills. Paul understood practice's essential nature and benefits and urged Timothy in that direction. Timothy would have to endure training Dionson (2015) described as intense, like an athlete preparing for the Olympic games. Timothy's training was to be so focused that he would not have time to dispute foolishness like fables. Instead, Timothy would commit wholeheartedly to reading, praying, meditating, and witnessing (MacDonald, 1990). Readers sense the intensity Paul wanted Timothy to adopt when he, in 2 Timothy 2:1, uses the analogy of soldiers in combat.

In the military comparison, MacDonald (1990) imagined a soldier during battles who would not have the time or energy to get entangled in civilian activities. Having the type of focused intensity Paul prescribed for Timothy would not come naturally – he would have to prepare himself. Evans and Holman (2019) understood that this type of preparation would not come about by physical exercise but would require Timothy to participate in practices leading to the development of godly actions, attitudes, and conduct.

Training was and still is an essential element in the growth of leaders. When Engstrom (1978) described the development of a church leader, he focused on the priority of training and education. He noted the resulting competence because of the instruction provided to leaders in training. During missionary journeys, Timothy witnessed how Paul disciplined his body (1 Corinthians 9:27), and now the exemplar tasked Timothy to do the same by training himself for godliness (v.7). Timothy's training as a leader came from watching Paul discipline himself and by Timothy emulating Paul's lifestyle.

The intensity of training caused toiling and striving to be a necessary addition to the leadership curriculum. For Timothy to achieve godliness, MacDonald (1990) stressed the acceptance of working through disappointment, while Evans and Holman (2019) emphasized enduring stressful times of hard work. According to Vine and Unger (1996), the path to godliness included extreme fatigue and disapproval periods. Why would Paul submit to such discomfort or expect Timothy to endure it? Cole (2005) suggested that when people understand the grave nature of people dying without Christ, there is no sacrifice too enormous for them to make if that sacrifice will correct the relationship or lack of relationship with God. Paul declared that he aggressively attempted to persuade folks because he understood God's fear (2 Corinthians 5:11). Paul explains why he toils and strives intensively while encouraging Timothy to persevere through all of life's misadventures. As we work through this discipleship process, one of our goals is for the learner to come to terms with the level of commitment required to continuously refine what God has placed in you and then take on the leadership tasks boldly.

Share God's Call on Your Life for Leadership

In the two recorded letters of Paul to Timothy, Paul repeatedly emphasized God's command and will as the authority for his leadership. Using those descriptors is how Paul began his pastoral letters to Timothy and those who would read the letter centuries later. Paul immediately established the source of his authority as God, and he also personalizes his fatherly relationship with Timothy by reminding him that he is his Spiritual son in the faith (Evans & Holman, 2019). With both authoritative positions stated, there are other times Paul reminded Timothy of who Paul was – not to intimidate Timothy but to inform him; not to maximize Timothy's confidence in Paul but to maximize Timothy's faith in Paul's source of authority. Paul stated that he was "an apostle of Christ Jesus by command of God" (*ESV*, 2001/2016, 1 Timothy 1:1), "appointed a preacher and an apostle" (*ESV*, 2001/2016, 1 Timothy 2:7), "an apostle of Christ Jesus by the will of God" (*ESV*, 2001/2016, 2 Timothy 2:1), and "appointed a preacher and apostle and teacher" (*ESV*, 2001/2016, 2 Timothy 2:11). Timothy had first-hand knowledge of Paul's modus operandi so Paul was confident Timothy would imitate him because Paul's life and message were different from the other teachers. Paul insisted that Timothy should be convinced because Timothy had witnessed God's hand at work in and through Paul (Idowu, 2017). Paul expressed and emphasized who he was so that Timothy would take note of his consistency and use it as a model for developing his identity with the Ephesian church.

One of the situations Timothy had seen Paul defending the source of his authority was with the Corinthian church. Forced into a defensive position, Paul went on the attack to protect the legitimacy of his ministry. Lambrecht (2001) described Paul's words as foolish talking because that is how Paul describes the lengths to which he had to go to make the case for his claims of apostleship. In 2 Corinthians 10-13, Paul went into excruciating, differentiating detail to distinguish himself from the false apostles and teachers in Corinth. In Paul's foolish writings to the Corinthian church, he made three noteworthy personal proclamations: morality, authority, and denial of inferiority (Lambrecht, 2001). It is instructive to know that leaders and teachers of that day made claims of their superiority to lord it over their subjects (Luke 22:25). At the same time, Paul expressed his position as an act of love to edify the church (2 Corinthians 13:10). Paul's expressions served as an example for Timothy to engage in and as a contingent expectation for those who would lead.

Timothy was going into a church already under the influence of teachers – uninformed, misinformed, and misinforming teachers, but teachers, nevertheless. Timothy's leadership responsibilities required him to speak up verbally and validate his talk with his walk. He would have to rebuke sinning elders (1 Timothy 5:20) and, in his preaching and teaching, "reprove, rebuke, and exhort, with complete patience" (2 Timothy 4:2). As the leading elder in the Ephesian church, Timothy would guide everyone in that fellowship, so Paul encouraged Timothy to speak boldly about life and doctrine. Paul wanted Timothy to imitate Jesus and emulate him. Evans and Holman (2019) and MacDonald (1990) agreed that the messages should focus on godliness, repentance, and faith. Campbell (1997) proposed that Timothy model the preaching content he heard from Paul, and Ituma et al. (2021) noted the boldness with which Timothy should make his proclamations. Whenever Timothy preached, Timothy had to overcome the challenges of his youth in the face of fatigue, disappointment, and disapproval. There were no guarantees of what Timothy would face as he assumed and executed his leadership role within the Ephesian church.

When you assume a leadership role within your place of worship, your entire head of hair, lack of facial hair, and youthful exterior and approach will likely come under attack. As we progress through this process, we will continue to extract from Paul's writing to his young protégé', Timothy, his guidance for navigating the waters of leadership, particularly leadership of seniors in age and experience. What qualifies a mere youth to manage, lead, and supervise a more experientially and technically advanced workforce than the leader? How should young leaders conduct themselves to gain and retain the respect required to influence followers to accomplish the mission? Paul's writings provide a viable way ahead whether the applicants consider themselves to be in the secular or spiritual domain.

The challenge of young people leading older people is not new. It biblically goes back to the twin births of Esau and Jacob when God said, "The older shall serve the younger" (*ESV*, 2001/2016, Genesis 25:23. Later, Joseph, Jacob's youngest son, dreamt of ruling over his siblings and having his siblings and parents bowing down to him. As the story progresses, we see Joseph's rise from the prison to the palace and a position of power over many people – including his parents. The Bible speaks of a millennial kingdom with naturally adversarial animals cohabitating and describes the governmental structure at that time, "A little child shall lead them." The Word of God is replete with leadership stories, many of which provide examples of the young leader-older follower phenomenon.

While these stories provide a biblical background, we can see similar instances in other venues. Every year, the military has Officers entering their ranks as Second Lieutenants, or Ensigns, who will immediately have senior enlisted military, and maybe civilians, reporting to them, relying on them to provide guidance, direction, and focus. A similar activity occurs each year when college graduates enter the job market. Some employees who have worked in retail venues for years receive their schedules, priorities, and assignments from newbies – recently hired employees hired into management positions. Your demanding task will be to lead God's people as you defend your hope and confront the uninformed, misinformed, and misinforming influencers within your sphere of worship. Andelin (1972) stated a truth applicable to all leaders and especially true for the learners who would lead when he noted the need for leaders to be both steel and velvet – strong of mind, fearless in assuming responsibility, and committed yet passionate, sensitive, loving, and compassionate towards those of lesser strength.

It is this type of leader Peter envisioned as strong and with convictions to defend yet compassionate and caring enough to do it "with gentleness and respect" (*ESV*, 2001/2016, 1 Peter 3:15). Know that challenges will come that you will have to quell. This process will prepare you to do it effectively.

MODULE ONE - LESSON THREE

IDENTIFYING THE CATEGORY OF CALLING

Overview

- The superhighway of leadership has numerous offramps.
- Square pegs do not fit in round holes.

Lesson Objectives

- To describe and assess areas of giftedness.
- To suggest avenues of service in leadership.

Scripture Readings

- 1 Timothy 2:7, 3:1, 8
- 2 Timothy 1:6, 11

Key Words

Deacon
Gift
Good Work

OVERVIEW

THE SUPERHIGHWAY OF LEADERSHIP

Leadership is a superhighway with numerous offramps for service in every possible venue at work, school, play, home, and church. People clamor for positions of greater authority and responsibility – some for the right reason, while others do so for selfish reasons. Our process is church-focused, so we turn our attention to the church. As far as the church is concerned, there are only two offices – elder and deacon. There seems to be quite a debate about whether there are two, three, or multiple leadership positions. For this course, we will briefly explore some other ideas, but we will conclude with two offices, elder and deacon, and focus our attention on the role of elder.

The term elder implies a person of many chronological years; however, the primary audience for this course is people in your age bracket – the youth. Although Scripture does not tell us how old Timothy was, tradition and Scripture imply he was a "youth" (*ESV*, 2001/2016, 1 Timothy 4:12). While listening to some music the other day, the artist described the people in the audience over the age of thirty-seven as old. Walker (2012), using various scenarios, posited Timothy's age to be between twenty-five and thirty. So, we will consider Timothy somewhere between the ages of twenty-one and thirty-seven for our purposes!

What makes the road to church leadership a superhighway since age is the only visible roadblock and there are only two exits? We will cover the complexities of the course in later modules as we examine the character, challenges, and charges of leadership. For now, we will assume your belief that God has called and caused you to travel a leadership road with two exits, and you intend to choose the elder exit.

SQUARE PEG, ROUND HOLE?

Years ago, a song advised that if it does not fit, do not force it. A famous idiomatic saying warned of the dangers of inserting or attempting to insert a square peg into a round hole. Makins and Isaacs (1991) explained the expression in terms of placing a person into a situation or position not suitable for that person. Sometimes, people attempt to get in where they do not fit, and at other times, they try to insert a person into a position or situation for which the insertee is uncomfortable. You have voluntarily inserted yourself into this process, and the process will help you determine if you are a fit.

The Word of God told the story of a person who was not the right fit or shape for the task. In 2 Samuel 18:19-33, someone had to run and deliver a message to King David, and Joab selected the Cushite to deliver the message. Before choosing the Cushite, another person, Ahimaaz, volunteered to deliver the news and would not be denied the privilege of running and delivering a message to David. Ahimaaz left after the Cushite but arrived at David's location before the Cushite. When he came, he gave David an incomplete, inaccurate message that caused David to put him aside - because he was not the right person to deliver the message. Then, the Cushite arrived and gave a complete and accurate statement that broke David's heart. The point here is that Ahimaaz had an excellent reputation (2 Samuel 18:27), a godly heritage as Zadok's son (2 Samuel 18:19), and he was a gifted, knowledgeable runner (2 Samuel 18:23). With all that going for him, Joab recognized that Ahimaaz was a square peg attempting to deliver a message into a round hole.

Like Timothy, you may have an incredible reputation, a godly heritage, and be genuinely gifted. The question is, should you travel the road to leadership or not? James's injunction is, "Not many of you should become teachers" (*ESV*, 2001/2016, James 3:1). In his analysis of this verse, Perkins (2020) put forth the possibility that James is seeking to eliminate those office seekers who are not qualified or are overly ambitious. Either way, leadership is not for everyone. Although a person may seem like a logical fit for responsibility (Ahimaaz), God has chosen the person He wants to run (Cushite). God chooses the appropriate vehicles for the leadership exit on the superhighway of leadership.

OBJECTIVES – LESSON THREE

ASSESS THE AREAS OF GIFTEDNESS

A common practice in sporting endeavors is to have team tryouts. Candidates will show up, and coaches will conduct various drills to determine strengths, weaknesses, skills, potential, and, ultimately, who will be on the team. Before any tryouts begin, the coaches have established standards by which they will assess the candidates. Sometimes, the standards are known, while at other times, the coaches may choose to keep their expectations and desires as close-hold items. Leaders of God's choosing may come into leadership via both channels. Let us briefly look at David (a close-hold selectee) and Paul (criteria-driven selectee).

After God brought Israel out of captivity and they became familiar with the nations God was allowing them to defeat, for some reason, Israel wanted to be led like those nations by a king – someone who would physically lead them into battle. Serving as God's prophet and the judge of the people, Samuel received instructions and appointed Saul as the first king of Israel. God's Word recorded that Saul was head and shoulders taller than the other people, and "There is none like him among all the people" (*ESV*, 2001/2016), 1 Samuel 10:24). When everyone saw Saul, he was physically an obvious choice for leader; however, Saul, full of himself, failed the obedience to God requirement causing Saul to have to anoint another king. So, when God sent Samuel to call a king from Jesse's sons, God told Samuel that He would show him the son of His choosing.

When Samuel saw the first son Jesse presented to him, he thought he was the one. Here is when God voiced how His close-hold selectee would come to light – God informed Samuel that looking at the appearance or height was how men made leadership determinations; however, "the Lord looks on the heart" (*ESV*, 2001/2016, 1 Samuel 16:7). David the son Jesse overlooked, was God's choice because he was a "man after His own heart" (*ESV*, 2001/2016, 1 Samuel 13:14; Acts 13:22). Saying God's criteria is close hold in this instance is because it was not apparent to man what God was looking for because different from their first king, David was not the evident choice height, appearance, or age. God sent Samuel on a search without specific requirements, restrictions, or rationale.

When God came after Saul, later Paul, God came directly for him. Scripture records multiple testimonies of Saul's conversion, all indicating the special requirements God desired. Keupfer (2009) narrowed the commonalities of the testimonies to 1) Paul's pre-conversion Pharisaic zeal, 2) the location on the road to Damascus from Jerusalem, 3) the powerful heavenly light that knocked Saul to the ground and blinded him, and 4) the get acquainted conversation between Jesus and Saul when Saul finally understood that it was Jesus he was persecuting. He concluded that God wanted this Pharisee to be His tool to declare the gospel's good news to the Gentiles (Keupfer, 2009). So, when God instructed Ananias to visit with Saul, Luke described Saul as God's "chosen instrument" (*ESV*, 2001/2016, Acts 9:15) to carry God's name to the Gentiles. God specifically chose a leader who formerly persecuted the church to be the source of expanding the church to the Gentile population. Paul recorded in Galatians 1:24 that when the Galatians understood his testimony and conversion, they acknowledged the power of God to change lives, which resulted in their praising God. In this instance, Paul's pre- and post-conversion reputations were significant in God's selection of Paul as a leader.

The point is that God has requirements for His leaders that He chooses to refine and redeem for His reasons. God is the source of the giftedness and the source of competence in the giftedness. In the referenced verse, Luke documented God's appointment, His requirement for Paul to be a preacher, an apostle, and a teacher of Gentiles. He did not independently assume the roles – they were God-appointed functions authorizing Paul to exercise leadership associated with the roles. In a way, Paul and Saul, Israel's first king, had something in common – authority from God. A significant difference was Saul's independent exercise of his authority and Paul's understanding that his "sufficiency [was] from God" (*ESV*, 2001/2016, 2 Corinthians 3:5). Paul wanted Timothy to know that the false teachers he was going to have to refute were independently attempting to replace God's authority with their blasphemous actions and allegations when they assumed God's authority to say and do things God had not said or required. Gleason (1997) stressed the importance of believers understanding God in the New Covenant as the source of Paul's adequacy because the New Covenant provided Paul with a new nature, which included "the desire and the ability to obey God" (p. 70). God appoints, approves, and improves those leaders who accept Him alone as their source of sufficiency and are willing to obey His directions.

You have voluntarily come to the tryout for church leadership. Our responsibility is to assess fitness and then assist you in determining how you fit in. Paul's journey, after conversion, took him to Arabia, where he saw the light, Damascus (Galatians 1:17-18). During this time, God allowed Paul to familiarize himself with the playbook and strengthen his Spiritual skills. As Paul wrote to Timothy, he used the metaphor of exercising to emphasize the relative importance of physical exercise to gaining Spiritual strength because the Ephesian culture understood the diligence required of athletes (Dionson, 2015). The same commitment required of athletes to be exceptional, Timothy would need to be effective in his work in the Ephesian church. Your challenge will be in the practical exercise of your calling as we require you to interact with the members of your congregation. You must work diligently to be on your "A" game. As Timothy's guide through the discipling process, Scholer (2016) emphasized the magnitude of Paul's efforts, guided by the Holy Spirit and empowered by God's grace, to overcome his past, which exceeded the efforts exerted by the other apostles. Paul's testimony was not degrading to the other apostles; he informed his readers of his commitment to excel and God's grace to excuse ignorance. Your hard work and commitment are areas we will consider more thoroughly when we progress to the "Challenges of Leadership" in module three.

Analyze Avenues of Service

We have uncovered that God's Word provided two offramps for leadership offices within the church – elders and deacons. While our focus here is on the office of elders, it will probably be instructive to touch briefly on deacons. An elder experiencing personal and congregational accountability issues deflected and defaulted on an area of an elder's responsibility. He pushed it off on the deacons without any personal thought or consideration of it being the responsibility of the elders. Many denominations have adopted traditions utilizing deacons in many ways; however, without seeking to condemn or commend, we will recount the expectations of deacons with minimal comment.

Deacons

Few question the origin of deacons coming out of the challenges in the early church Luke described in Acts 6. Strauch (2009) conjectured the Seven as the prototype for deacons Paul would later label in 1 Timothy. Clarke (2007) and Willimon (2016) provided detailed connections between the Seven and the responsibilities Paul specified in 1 Timothy 3 by recognizing the deacons as supporting and serving leaders charged with essential tasks that they must accomplish with diligence and efficiency.

When MacDonald (1990) made the same connection, he described the deacon's role as that of a servant "who cares for the temporal affairs of the local church" (p. 904). He differentiated the deacon's role from that of an elder by noting the elders were to take care of the Spiritual needs of the body (MacDonald, 1990). The distinction is highlighted by the apostles when they determined the necessity of the Seven to take care of the physical needs of the church so that they could focus on "prayer and the ministry of the Word" (*ESV*, 2001/2016, Acts 6:4). Each role required execution in servant-leader mode where the leaders served God as they served and led the people – deacons in the physical realm while elders primarily focused on the Spiritual realm.

The Seven specifically served in a capacity that freed the apostles to tend to other tasks. So, when Paul described the characteristics of the men who would be deacons, he focuses more on character than on missions. MacDonald (1990) commented on the similarity of qualifications for elders and deacons by noting the areas of dissimilarity – deacons do not have the requirement to be "able to teach" (*ESV*, 2001/2016, 1 Timothy 3:2) or to manage the business of the church (1 Timothy 3:5). While they did not have the specific task to teach, Scripture pointed out that must "hold the mystery of the faith with a clear conscience" (*ESV*, 2001/2016, 1 Timothy 3:9) which Evans and Holman (2019) posited meant that deacons had to have a firm grasp on and grounding in Christian doctrine. People would know that they have the grip and grounding because not only would the deacons know doctrine, but their lifestyles would also give evidence of their knowledge (MacDonald, 1990).

Elders

The other exit from the church leadership freeway is for the office of elders. Paul's directive to Titus was that he "appoint elders in every town" (*ESV*,

2001/2016, Titus 1:5). Timothy was to determine the quality of the men in the Ephesian church who aspired to eldership (1 Timothy 3:1). In his letters to Timothy and Titus, Paul provided the qualifications for serving as an elder, and in describing the qualifications, he also defined their role in the church – to provide Spiritual oversight of the local church. Strauch (2009) combined the definition and description of eldership by noting that elders "oversee, lead, and care for the local church" (p. 2) by preaching and teaching the Word, protecting the flock from false doctrines, and visiting and praying for the sick.

While the characteristics of the elder and deacon were similar, the elders had two duties distinguishing them from the deacons – one specified (teaching) and the other implied (managing). As Paul detailed godly qualities required of elders, he included as a distinctive that the elder must be "able to teach" (*ESV*, 2001/2016, 1 Timothy 3:2). Being able to teach means that the elder must be able to present God's Word in an understandable method that makes plain to the audience the truths of Scripture. Mayhue (2011) highlighted this competency as one that moves beyond having the motivation to teach versus the ability to communicate and apply biblical doctrine. Peter's pride stimulated him to speak up for the cause of Christ in Luke 22:33, but he failed miserably by denying Christ three times shortly after that (Luke 22:54-62). There is a new, empowered, and enabled Peter who can deliver truth in his speaking after Pentecost (Mayhue, 2011). Peter's initial efforts were self-generated; however, Paul's instruction to Timothy was for him "to present [himself] to God" to be able to "rightly [handle] the Word of truth" (*ESV*, 2001/2016, 2 Timothy 2:15). As an elder, one must commit to diligent, intensive studying to be able to apply the Word accurately and relevantly. Glasscock (1987) added that being able to teach may have also addressed the teachability of the elders. Even as Paul was approaching his life's end, he requested that Timothy bring him materials, books, and parchments to study and share God's Word (MacDonald, 1990). An elder's ongoing and enduring preparation enables a clear defense of the gospel while the Holy Spirit empowers its delivery.

In addition to having and developing teaching skills, Paul wrote that the elders are responsible for managing God's church. The qualifications for eldership mandated that the candidate be a good household manager, including keeping his children in check. Here is where Paul parenthetically questioned the ability of a man to "care for God's church" (*ESV*, 2001/2016, 1 Timothy 3:5). Managing the household well was an indicator of the ability to manage church affairs and a prerequisite for selection (Strauch, 2009). Evans and Holman (2019) emphasized that managing well does not preclude issues and problems from arising; however, the elder's strength must be in recognizing the case, taking responsibility, and then working to address the matter biblically. When integrating the Gentile believers into the church, the apostles and the elders gathered, considered, debated, and made a judgment (Acts 15:6-19) that they communicated to the Gentile believers. MacDonald (1990) described the elderly duty as managing, taking care of, and shepherding the local body of believers without any thought of ruling over them in a dictatorial sense. The Greek Word Paul used, and Clark (2006) clarified is sometimes translated to manage or oversee to indicate a level of personal involvement in household and family development, unlike the leaders who, in a hierarchical sense, dominated people's lives.

The ability to reason with people is at the intersection of teaching/ preaching and managing. Since God is willing to "reason together" with humanity, why would we not be ready to reason with one another (*ESV*, 2001/2016, Isaiah 1:18)? As Timothy traveled with Paul on numerous occasions, he witnessed Paul reasoning with people vice becoming engaged with them in an argument – Paul reasoned with the Thessalonians from Scripture (Acts 17:2); Paul reasoned in the synagogue with the Jews (Acts 17:17); in Corinth, Paul reasoned in the synagogue with Jews and Greeks (Acts 18:4); and, Paul reasoned with the Jews in Ephesus in the temple and the pagan unbelievers in the hall of Tyrannus (Acts 18:19, 19:8-9). Reasoning avoided with people was a way of avoiding arguments, contention, and strife. Culpepper (1986) posited that the compliant nature of reasoning avoided stubbornness and being unyielding – open to debate without compromising the truth. As the leader of the Ephesian church, Timothy would have to protect the flock from false teachers by countering their efforts with "complete patience and teaching" (*ESV*, 2001/2016, 2 Timothy 4:2). Timothy's behavior, then, would be an example of modeling for those who chose the elder exit of what it looked like to be intentionally gentle when resolving conflicts and avoiding heated discussions of minor to no consequence.

Now, as in the early church, some will take the elder exit whose lifestyles warrant eldership, and their ability to rule well merits additional consideration. If that describes you, you will be delighted as you recall Paul's words to Timothy: "Let the elders who rule well be considered worthy of double honor, especially those who labor in preaching and teaching" (*ESV*, 2001/2016, 1 Timothy 5:17). This is probably a topic for a later date, but you need to have an awareness of it now. Because of his audience and to demonstrate God's power to use that which people look down on, Paul called preaching foolishness (1 Corinthians 1:21); however, Jesus specified that His Father sent Him to earth for the purpose – to "preach the good news of the *ESV*, 2001/2016, Luke 4:43). All elders must have the ability to teach. However, there are those whom God has gifted to teach and preach. While many use the terms interchangeably, there is a difference that Dodd (1944) pointed out – preaching is missionary (evangelistic) in its purpose with the world as its primary audience, while teaching is ethical (edifying) with the church as its primary audience. MacDonald (1990) pointed to the necessity of preaching to the lost, Jews and Gentiles, the message of salvation – the basis of the Christian missionary movement. On the other hand, the proclamation known as the Sermon on the Mount, beginning in Matthew 5, was a teaching session delivered by Jesus as He sat down.

Elders are responsible for managing church business governmentally and Spiritually; however, some have the desire and ability to accurately and effectively communicate the gospel to a lost and dying world.

For those of you choosing the exit of eldership, the ability to teach is a non-negotiable requirement. Rowe (1999) described effective teaching as engaging the students and causing them to desire to imitate the instruction. Paul considered his calling to be a preacher, apostle, and teacher (1 Timothy 2:7; 2 Timothy 1:11), yet throughout his letters to Timothy, he repeatedly emphasized teaching, urging Timothy's ongoing study so that in his teaching he might "rightly [handle] the Word of truth" (*ESV*, 2001/2016, 2 Timothy 2:15). Rightly handling the Word involves the teacher's study of the Word as well as the teacher's delivery of the Word to the students. Stevens (1985) provided extensive methodologies for ensuring teaching would be appropriate and practical, with the goal being to launch the students into "revelation-centered and quality characterized ministry for Jesus Christ" (p. 17). Inconsistencies will marginalize your effectiveness as a teacher when the life you portray and the gospel your lips proclaim are not in sync.

MODULE 2

THE CHARACTER OF LEADERSHIP

MODULE INTRODUCTION

Welcome to the second module of the FMIFC curriculum process. In this module, we will be covering the Character of Leadership. Again, we will focus on Paul's writings to Timothy and the character requirements of godly leaders. There are always expectations placed upon leaders, which is especially true of the leaders in the church because the expectations come from God. We will begin by defining godly character, move on to methodologies for assessing your character, and conclude with some recommended approaches for strengthening the quality of your character. Below is an overview of the content we will cover during this segment.

Module Two Overview

	Lesson One: Defining Character	**Lesson Two:** Assessing the Content of My Character	**Lesson Three:** Developing the Godly Quality of My Character
Overview:	* Godly character is an imperative for godly leadership. * There is a difference between good character and godly character. * Leaders must lead by modeling.	* Leaders must be aware of their blind spots and be willing to be accountable and hold others accountable. * God's Word provides the standard for character assessment.	* The leader's practice must match the leader's preaching. * Leaders get better by persistently practicing the principles of God's Word. * The Spiritual development of the leader is an ongoing activity.
Objectives:	* To define and describe "character." * To determine the importance of character for godly leadership. * To delve into a model of godly character.	* To compare Spiritual growth with departures from Spiritual growth. * To acknowledge areas for growth and development.	* To allow the Holy Spirit to guide in Spiritual growth and development. * To anticipate the benefits of perseverance through challenging times.
Scripture Readings:	1 Timothy 1:12, 6:8, 11, 2 Timothy 1:7, 2:2, 10	1 Timothy 1:12, 19-20, 2:7, 3:7, 5:1-2, 6:8, 11, 21, 2 Timothy 1:7, 15, 2:2, 10, 17, 3:12, 4:10	1 Timothy 1:12, 4:6, 5:1-2, 6:8, 11, 2 Timothy 1:4, 7, 2:2, 10, 25, 3:12, 4:7, 11, 16
Vocabulary/Key Words:	Faithful, content, righteousness, godliness, steadfastness, gentleness, love, self-control	Reputation, endurance	Servant, joy, teacher, forgiveness

MODULE TWO – LESSON ONE

DEFINING CHARACTER

OVERVIEW

- Godly character is an imperative for godly leadership.
- There is a difference between good character and godly character.
- Leaders must lead by modeling.

LESSON OBJECTIVES

- To define and describe "character."
- To determine the importance of character for godly leadership.
- To delve into a model of godly character.

SCRIPTURE READINGS

- 1 Timothy 1:12, 6:8, 11
- 2 Timothy 1:7, 2:2, 10

KEY WORDS

Faithful	Steadfastness
Content	Gentleness
Righteousness	Love
Godliness	Self-Control

OVERVIEW

CHARACTER – THE GODLY IMPERATIVE

First and foremost, God desires leaders who will emulate His character so that He gets the glory from their actions, attitudes, and assertions. God's measurement extends beyond the physical attributes commonly used to determine who should be a leader. When Northouse (2019) summarized leadership descriptors, he narrowed it down to identifying leaders based on physical traits (height, intelligence, personality) or how the leader interacts with followers. Both models initially focus on what the human senses determine and subsequently on the leader's character and ethicality. We will spend some time defining character later in this instruction, but for now, think of character as who a person is on the inside – where no human can inerrantly make an assessment. Pojman (1995) described an individual's nature as ingrained in the virtues rooted in a person's heart. His description is consistent with Jeremiah's proclamation of the heart's deceitfulness that only God can search and know (Jeremiah 17:9-10). It explains Samuel's declaration to Saul that God "has sought out a man after His own heart" (*ESV*, 2001/2016, 1 Samuel 13:14). When God sent Samuel to anoint Israel's next king, He did not send him to the tallest, the oldest, or wisest of Jesse's sons; He caused Samuel to look beyond the exterior and guided him to the virtuous son who would allow God to guide his actions, attitudes, and assertions.

Because God is looking at the heart, process-focused leaders who positively interact with their followers may also not be God's choice for a leader. Solomon wrote of a man whose actions, attitudes, and assertions indicated he was generous; however, his character – who he was on the inside- identified him as disingenuous (Proverbs 23:6-7). After arguing against the common understanding of the Proverbs 23:6-7 passage, Barker (1989) posited that how a host serves food within himself reveals his character and motivation. From the outside looking in, he is doing a service that benefits those under his care. When God views the meal, He notes a facade of generosity and unselfish sharing covering a deceitful, desperately wicked heart that begrudges those served. God is looking for leaders with character – those with a heart fully committed to godly actions, attitudes, and assertions. Northouse (2019) asserted that people can learn noble character from others but noted ethicality as essential for a leader to effectively influence those who follow. Christian leaders must have, develop, and demonstrate godly character. It is a non-negotiable imperative for leadership.

Good Character versus Godly Character

The prerequisite for a Christian leader is godly character and not simply good character. When a person aspires to a leadership role within the body of Christ, there must be a commitment to becoming like Christ inside and out. Those who are simply good are not good enough. Isaiah, speaking for God, said all the good things they were doing amounted to filthy rags in God's sight (Isaiah 64:6). Blank (1952) expanded the thought of actions to the virtues that guided the actions and noted that it was the virtues that humanity accepts and classifies as meritorious that are not acceptable, not good enough. When Northouse (2019) traced the historical references to ethical behavior, he returned to Plato and Aristotle.

He described the virtuosity of a person in terms of what an individual or society deems desirable or appropriate for a given situation. The Pharisees would be at the pinnacle of self-righteous people with good character who prided themselves in keeping and enforcing the Mosaic laws. Jesus clarified that a person's righteousness would have to exceed that of the Pharisees to make it to heaven. After delivering that shocking statement to the people, Jesus went on to provide examples for the people of what comprised godly expectations as He differentiated between what the people accepted as righteousness when He declared, "But I say to you" (*ESV*, 2001/2016, Matthew 5:22,27, 32, 34, 39, 44). The scribes and Pharisees had a standard they prescribed for the people and pretended to live up to, but God's assessment determined that their best attempts, like your best efforts, would inevitably fall short of God's requirement.

Leaders Lead by Modeling

We have noted the necessity of leaders providing a model worthy of emulation, and we cannot overemphasize the point. Northouse (2019) defined leaders as those influencing individuals and groups to accomplish a common goal while noting the interconnectedness of leading and following. Whether a leader comes to a position via leadership traits or through a leadership process, they were followers or learners at some point. In his letter to the Corinthians, Paul invited the Corinthian believers to imitate him but only as he imitated Christ (1 Corinthians 11:1). Paul's invitation should be the mantra of all Christian leaders as an offer to accountability with those following and to themselves as a measuring rod for effectiveness. When Paul wrote to Timothy, providing him with guidance and instructions, there was an expectancy of compliance on Paul's part. Timothy should follow the teachings he had grown up with and those he heard and saw while on mission trips with Paul (Veiss, 2018).

In the past, Timothy's mother and grandmother had introduced him to the "sacred writing" (*ESV*, 2001/2016, 2 Timothy 3:15) that pointed him to salvation. After being saved, he witnessed God at work in Paul's "teaching, conduct, life, faith, patience, love, steadfastness, in persecutions and sufferings" (*ESV*, 2001/2016, 2 Timothy 3:10-11).

Consequently, Veiss (2018) concluded that these personal character experiences would carry forward into Timothy's life and ministry. A result of Timothy's exposure to godly character is that he could identify the holy character in other "faithful men" (*ESV*, 2001/2016,2 Timothy 2:2), who would continue the tradition of teaching and training others of godly character. For God-influenced succession to occur, it begins with having character, modeling character, identifying character, and then training those identified with character to prepare others to take up the mantle.

OBJECTIVES: LESSON ONE

Define and Describe Character

In Academia, many words describe our topic of character, yet two leaders provide the practical perspective desired for you to be an effective leader. John Wooden provides the first description when he differentiates between character and reputation. Wooden and Jamison (2005), even in the sporting world, were more concerned with your character than reputation and sought to maximize opportunities to develop inner awareness in the athletes as they competed against their best selves. There was little concern for external assessments because the players focused on being the best versions of themselves while seeking to maximize their capabilities (Wooden & Jamison, 2005). People with character know themselves and focus on maximizing their ability to achieve and improve on their personal best efforts. They are aware of external happenings without concentrating on them for comparison purposes. As a Christian leader, the Holy Spirit provides you with your inner compass and scale for measurement. Jesus stated that one of the Holy Spirit's responsibilities was to lead and guide into all truth (John 16:13). What is the possibility of the Holy Spirit being slack in doing His work? As leaders of God's people, we must be attentive and obedient to the Holy Spirit's promptings.

We will hear and obey urgently when we understand the importance of demonstrating character. Jamieson et al. (1997) portrayed character as the proof of desirable personal qualities – proof indicative of a past tense occurrence for which one can provide evidence. When writing of the required qualities of leadership, Maxwell (2001) quoted Billy Graham, one of the most noted and trusted preachers of God's Word, "When wealth is lost, nothing is lost; when health is lost, something is lost; when character is lost, all is lost." A loss of character indicates a minimization of the Holy Spirit's influence in one's life. To avoid this tragic occurrence, Paul urged Timothy to be a man devoted to an outward display of the inner guidance he was receiving. Timothy was to "train [himself] for godliness" (*ESV*, 2001/2016, 1 Timothy 4:7) because of its benefits for him and those who would follow him. A life well lived is proof of character, but what does that look like while one is living?

Paul provided an answer when he described his co-worker, Timothy. Paul depicted Timothy to the church at Philippi as a one-of-a-kind person with genuine love and concern for the welfare of others. Paul could write this confidently because evidence revealed Timothy had "proven worth" (*ESV*, 2001/2016, Philippians 2:22). He had served side-by-side with Paul, repeatedly performing selfless acts of integrity, caring, and courage. You can label yourself as having character; however, time, challenging situations, and people will reveal the depth of your sincerity. Paul provided Timothy with character-defining qualities required for those who, like you, aspire to leadership:

1 Timothy 3:2

- Above reproach – Cannot be successfully accused of wrongdoing. The leader must be prepared to lead in the community, family, and the church. There is a high standard he must uphold, requiring him to be blameless, a clear thinker, and disciplined.
- Sober-minded – Must be a clear thinker.
- Self-controlled – Has his desires under control to make reasoned decisions.
- Respectable – He is worthy of respect.

1 Timothy 3:3

- Not a drunkard – Must not lose control to intoxicating substances. He cannot be addicted to any mind-altering substance - drug or alcohol that might cause him to be violent or quarrelsome. He is responsible for being gentle while avoiding heated discussions about matters of little to no consequence. While he will need money to manage his household, he does not think of money as a source but rather a resource God provides because he cannot love God and money (Matt. 6:24).
- Not violent – Not given to violent confrontations but intentionally gentle when resolving conflict.
- Not quarrelsome – Able to gently resolve conflicts he did not initiate and avoids pointless quarrels.
- Not a lover of money – The leader cannot think money solves every problem.

1Timothy 3:4

- Manage his household well – Speaks to his ability to judge rightly. A leader must be someone like Abraham, who will "command his children and household after him" to do things God's way (Genesis 18:19). As the overseer, he must also act as the spiritual leader in the household, having the responsibility to instruct the children without provoking them to anger (Ephesians 6:4).

1 Timothy 3:6

- Humble – A leader must not think more highly of himself than merited. A significant problem here is pride of position. We do not know anything of the devil's accomplishments - only that he was beautiful and occupied a high visibility position (Ezekiel 28; Isaiah 14) until his pride got the best of him. Pride would especially be problematic for a novice.

These qualities are non-negotiable, and the leader must have them ever-increasingly. To slip in one area is an across-the-board loss; as Billy Graham stated, that would be a total loss. The FMIFC process aims to produce godly, young leaders; however, there is a significant difference between being young and being new – young, not new!

Determine the Importance of Character for Godly Leadership

A popular saying years ago was, "God said it, I believe it, that settles it!" If God said it, it is settled and requires no further agreement, discussion, or consideration. Jesus was different from the leaders and teachers of His day in that He presented His instruction authoritatively (Matthew 7:29). After living amongst the people and teaching them, Jesus gathered followers around Him and provided education and examples, empowering them to have supernatural power and authority. There were many lessons He taught His followers before releasing them to the masses; however, there are two traits the FMIFC process will focus on here to emphasize their practice for effective godly leadership – being authentic and having discernment.

Authenticity

Timothy was going to be ministering in a city with many false teachers. They were spreading incorrect doctrine ignorantly. Evans and Holman (2019) described the teachers as proud people pretending to know the law that they did not truly understand. Their teachings mixed grace with the law, promoted the insufficiency of faith, and were harmful to themselves and their adherents (MacDonald, 1990). Nothing was genuine about these teachers – who they were, what they taught, or their knowledge of the material. Timothy's mission was to clean up what they had messed up. Timothy was to lovingly end these teachings and carry out his role as a man of character – with "a pure heart and a good conscience and a sincere faith" (*ESV*, 2001/2016, 1 Timothy 1:5). Then he would be able to refute the false teaching and replace those teachings with the truth by providing an understanding of the relationship of the law to grace. Paul told Timothy that by consistently living out the truths he taught, everyone would note his progress and benefit Timothy and those hearing him.

Paul did not want Timothy to become like the scribes, the Pharisees, or the other leaders of that time. Jesus's teachings were authoritative because of His talk and walk consistency. Donahue (2002) highlighted Jesus's controversial condemnation of the Pharisees who preached but did not practice, loved to have exalted titles and positions of authority, and were consistently inconsistent with how they lived their lives compared to their expectations of others. In these days of leaders carrying themselves like chameleons and compromising in areas where there should be resistance, your effectiveness as a leader will come to light as you become more and more like Jesus. The consistent authenticity of your character will separate you from the pretenders who are tossed about by every wind of doctrine (Ephesians 4:14) and leading their followers astray. People need to be able to see and hear the real deal to distinguish between the false and the factual and that which is counterfeit and that which is credible.

Discernment

How good are you at distinguishing between what is good and which is the best? How about distinguishing between good and evil? While the latter decision seems easy to determine, think about how you would respond if you were Solomon and had to decide between the two women written about in 1 Kings 3. Solomon had just prayed to "discern between good and evil" (*ESV*, 2001/2016, 1 Kings 3:9). One of the women had good intentions, and the other had evil intentions. They were both prostitutes and provided Solomon with plausible stories. Solomon's request of God was to have the ability to put his understanding in overdrive. Humans understand with their minds; however, discernment is the understanding one receives through the "divine mode" of the Holy Spirit (Dingeldein, 2013, p. 32). All spiritual believers have the "mind of Christ" (*ESV*, 2001/2016, 1 Corinthians 2:16). Still, God has given specially gifted people to the church to prepare them to do the work of ministry and to build up other believers (Ephesians 4:11-12). This special enablement is available when leaders like Solomon ask God to give them what they need to lead His people.

As a young man with a divine assignment, Timothy would need a special anointing of discernment to effectively take on the Ephesian church's challenges. Lawson (2002) provided the backdrop for why Timothy's commitment to his assignment would be humanly challenging – Timothy was young, going into a church that had not requested his presence, and had several wealthy congregants prepared to pounce on a Timid Timothy. So, in private practice, Timothy, through the Holy Spirit, would experience the enhanced and empowered enablement for public proclamation. The Holy Spirit would enable him to encourage older men as fathers, "younger men as brothers, older women as mothers, [and] younger women as sisters (*ESV*, 2001/2016, 1 Timothy 5:1-2). Kleinig (2017) described what the Holy Spirit would give Timothy as the ability to be sound in his thinking. Timothy would have a clear mind about who he was, who the people he was leading were, and how to communicate with them effectively (Kleining, 2017). Without Spiritual discernment, Timothy's words and actions could be misunderstood and misinterpreted by the followers.

An associate of mine once told me, "You can have the best idea in the world, but it is of no use if you do not communicate it in the language of your audience." Since you have access to the Holy Spirit, you would do well to ask for guidance, listen for His response, and then carry out the directions in the prescribed manner. Some see the challenge as determining if the suggestion in my mind is from the Spirit or a random idea. Jesus cautioned His followers that trying times would cause them not to know what to do or say and that they should be "Wise as serpents and innocent as doves" (*ESV*, 2001/2016, Matthew 10:16). The discourse in Matthew 10 continued with Jesus informing the apostles that the Spirit would speak through them. Porter (1987) inferred from Jesus's words that they were, as wise serpents, to be situationally aware of their audience so that they could discern what to say and say it with the innocence of a dove. Similar situations sometimes require different approaches. Here is one to consider from Proverbs 26:4-5 – responding to a fool. At first glance, Solomon plays both sides against the middle and gives contradictory advice. Upon reflection, Solomon advises the exercise of discernment – the very thing he asked God for at the start of his reign as king. There are several factors involved in developing a discerning spirit. While focusing on remaining humble and avoiding hypocrisy, we will detail some of those factors as we delve into a person with a godly character.

DELVE INTO A MODEL OF GODLY CHARACTER

In this story of succession, we see Paul providing words of wisdom and instruction to his disciple, Timothy, having traveled extensively with him and observing his manner of living. While many godly people are on the pages of Scripture, none seem more appropriate currently than Paul. We will examine Paul's life as expressed in his writings to Timothy and see how his life bore out his teaching. For simplicity, we will categorize Paul's godly character under two headings – Remaining Humble and Avoiding Hypocrisy, all under the worthy banner of Imitation.

Remaining Humble

There are things about us that make us stand out from the crowd in a way that exalts us over them. Superior intelligence, good looks, riches, or some other physical feature may be a source of pride in our lives. Pride is not limited to the physical realm because it may also appear in a person's spiritual life. Our model, Paul, had the privilege of experiencing the "third heaven" (*ESV*, 2001/2016, 2 Corinthians 12:2), and God gave him a physical ailment "to keep [him] from becoming conceited" (*ESV*, 2001/2016, 2 Corinthians 12:7). We also know from Daniel's experience with Nebuchadnezzar that God can humble those who are proud. Paul did not take pride in his conversion experience or the challenges of life he encountered because of his conversion. Instead, he used those experiences to describe his actions and the motive generating his actions honestly.

Finally, in this section, we will explore a path of discernment to enable a response versus a reaction.

Honesty. Paul was not bashful about who he was before meeting Christ on the road to Damascus. He made sure Timothy knew that in the past, he had been a "blasphemer, persecutor, and insolent opponent" (*ESV*, 2001/2016, 1 Timothy 1:13) of the church. Knowing that he excelled in those roles made Paul understand the abundance of God's grace and kept him humble. Every time Paul gave his testimony, he honestly presented his checkered past as an example of the depth and reach of God's grace and mercy (Evans & Holman, 2019). Benjamin Franklin received credit for coining the phrase, "Honesty is the best policy," and those who would be leaders of God's people would do well to adopt honesty as the only policy.

Love. In his letter to the Corinthian church, Paul dedicated a section detailing what love is and what love does. Timothy was going to a church with many false teachers – people who espoused a "different doctrine" (*ESV*, 2001/2016, 1 Timothy 1:3) from what Timothy had heard Paul preach and teach. Among the many challenging communications Paul had to deliver to the churches, Paul had to deal with immorality in the Corinthian church and false teaching in Galatia and Colossae. Timothy would face similar situations in Ephesus that he would have to speak to. The driving motivation for having the corrective discussions had to be love from a pure heart and sincere faith – a spirit of authenticity. As the writer of Hebrews 12:6 noted, discipline and correction come from the fruit of love. If God did not love us, He would not discipline us. Paul's corrective measures with the churches had love as their motive, and Paul encouraged Timothy to have the same motivation as he led the Ephesian church. Paul equated action without love as a non-accomplishment.

Discernment. Earlier, we noted the difference between understanding and discernment using the Dingeldein (2013) description of discernment as understanding acquired from the Holy Spirit in a spiritual communication versus a mental communication completed in one's mind. Paul understood the shortfall of mental understanding when doing God's work and insisted that a renewed sense of reasoning was necessary. Bryant (2004) explained the renewal process as a work of the Holy Spirit that causes a person to accept and receive a new way of living and thinking that enables them to discern what conforms with God's will. Still, the question arises as to how this process flows. Here are some verses for consideration – James 1:19-20.

If one is to acquire wisdom from the Holy Spirit, step one is to listen. Listen to the person communicating their situation to you. Covey (2020) clarified that the primary key to effective communication is understanding, which you cannot do if you do not listen. This listening must be for understanding and not for preparing a response. James prioritized listening, and as you listen to understand, the Holy Spirit will communicate truths to you that require your attentiveness to the promptings of the Holy Spirit. We know that you are not listening primarily to respond because James advised slowness of speech, a deliberate response to what has entered your spirit and been refined by the Spirit. Garland (1986) posited that restraint of speech causes leaders to mind their speech and not just speak their minds, especially in a manner that does not glorify God or build up His people. Understanding that the evidence of God's righteousness is the priority, one must think about what causes anger after listening quickly as a part of restraining speech. Paul wrote to the Ephesians that they were to be angry, but the additional injunction was that their anger was not to be a source of sin. There was to be an anger of a righteous sort (Ephesians 4:26). Garland (1986) reminded readers that irritation, when left unchecked, can result in irreparable damage, is the first step to murder, and can destroy us and those around us.

When facing the eminent difficulties of leadership, the discernment only the Holy Spirit can provide is essential. Take courage in knowing that as those times occur, God has given you the spirit of a sound mind, and as Paul shared with Timothy, "The Lord will give you understanding in everything" (*ESV*, 2001/2016, 2 Timothy 2:7). The challenge in discernment is in doing. What you have heard from the Spirit needs to be evidenced in your conduct.

Avoiding Hypocrisy

When I think of hypocrisy, I think of using a covering to alter the authentic appearance of that which has the cover. Vine and Unger (1996) and Strong (2009) referred to hypocrisy as acting in a feigned role to deceive. Think of Jacob covering his hands and neck with goatskins to deceive his father, Isaac, into thinking he was his older son, Esau. The essence is the same as the wolves who would come dressed in sheep's clothing. They would deceptively do whatever is needed to acquire what was not rightfully theirs.

Conversely, the hymn writer Charlotte Elliott wrote of coming to Jesus "Just As I Am" without any pretense. Paul did not sugarcoat what it was like to be a leader of God's people but noted that the internal formation of Christ was a process that came with many physical, mental, and spiritual challenges. Timothy had the benefit of assessing Paul's life in real-time and the opportunity to imitate Paul as Paul imitated Christ.

Suffering. Sometimes, people disguise what they are going through because they think it will encourage others to walk in their pathway. They do not want to discourage others. Our model, Paul, did not want to discourage Timothy but did not want to give him false expectations of the road ahead. He told him plainly that the road included toiling, striving (1 Timothy 4:10), and suffering (2 Timothy 1:12; 2:9-10). He wanted Timothy to be prepared for the journey because he knew that the byproduct of endurance was character development – the building of godly character (Romans 5:4). Taking the mask off is not a tactic to scare someone but to allow them to view reality unfiltered to adjust their level of expectation management appropriately.

Intentions. Saint Bernard of Clairvaux received credit for stating, "The road to hell is paved with good intentions." Intentions are the deep-seated motivations undergirding actions and activities that one must discern through thoughtful contemplation. James stated that God's Word could distinguish between the "thoughts and the intentions of the heart" (*ESV*, 2001/2016, James 4:12). God's Word looks beyond the deed, understands the underlying motivation for action, and after making that distinction, "judges us" (MacDonald, 1990, p. 985). When a person hears the clear preaching of the Word and comes under conviction, Evans and Holman (2019) credited the conviction to the power of God's Word, cutting through all that is false and exposing us to God.

Paul made sure that Timothy knew what right looked and sounded like. The Ephesian false, hypocritical teachers were promulgating false doctrines consisting of myths, genealogies, and speculations that they confidently and incorrectly attributed to the law. Paul's discernment enabled him to see that these fake teachers with law masks were saying things that captured the weak and immature people and trapped them in a learning mode with the knowledge button disabled (2 Timothy 3:6-7). Evans and Holman (2019) described the mask of the false teachers who externally projected religious devotion but were devoid of God's power and approval – "religion masquerading as godliness" (p. 1296). Timothy witnessed Paul teaching the true gospel and would now have the written reminder.

Conclusion - Imitation

It would be great if Paul had the ongoing mission to disciple young leaders. He could lead them on mission trips as he did Timothy. He could use them as messengers to various churches as he did with Timothy. He could allow them to participate in written communications to the churches as he did with Timothy. Paul would encourage them to imitate his life patterns like he was an imitator of Jesus Christ (1 Corinthians 11:1). Eight times in his letters to the churches, Paul solicited imitation of Jesus or him. MacDonald (1990) characterized the imitation as copying Christ. Bruce (1980) provided the extra details of Paul choosing to imitate Christ over his contemporaries, who were less considerate of those with lower levels of maturity and enlightenment. Paul saw the value in Christlikeness, so in his life, he was attentive to remaining humble, avoiding hypocrisy, and did as he told Timothy: "Keep a close watch on yourself and on the teaching…by so doing you will save both yourself and your hearers" (*ESV*, 2001/2016, 1 Timothy 4:16). As you do all the things worthy of emulation, make love your catalyst for action.

MODULE TWO – LESSON TWO

ASSESSING THE CONTENT OF MY CHARACTER

OVERVIEW

- Leaders must be aware of their blind spots and be willing to be accountable and hold others accountable.
- God's Word provides the standard for character assessment.

LESSON OBJECTIVES

- To compare Spiritual growth with departures from Spiritual growth.
- To acknowledge areas for growth and development.

SCRIPTURE READINGS

- 1 Timothy 1:12, 19-20, 2:7, 3:7, 5:1-2, 6:8, 11, 21
- 2 Timothy 1:7, 15, 2:2, 10, 17, 3:12, 15-17, 4:10

Key Words

Reputation
Endurance

OVERVIEW

Blind Spots and Accountability

One of the challenges of leadership is the responsibility of decision-making. Everyone makes decisions because life is all about making decisions; however, the decisions leaders make impact at the leader's organizational level. As humanity's federal head and the head of his family, the results of Adam's decision to allow Eve to eat the forbidden tree changed the course of humanity for all time. Through the prophet Jeremiah, God assessed the actions of His leaders as "stupid" and causing His people to be "scattered" (*ESV*, 2001/2016, Jeremiah 10:21). While some leaders are devious and have wicked intentions, sometimes leaders make poor decisions unwittingly. Either they do not have all the information, or because of some impediment, they overlook essential elements. Zaccaro et al. (2000) pointed to the need for leaders to go beyond the information given to them and to consider unique solutions – solutions obscured by the leader's blind spots.

Leaders do not see or consider those solutions because they are in their blind spots. Bazerman and Tenbrunsel (2011) describe an individual blind spot as the gap between who you want to be and who you are. The indiscretions or poor choices are not intentional or nefarious; instead, they are choices by "culpably ignorant" people engaged in behaviors that seem all right (Bazerman & Tenbrunsel, 2011, p. 3). When they become knowledgeable of the same behavior in another person, the error is more evident than when they carry on in the same manner. The specific problem is one of what Bazerman and Tenbrunsel (2011) labeled "bounded awareness," which limits one's ability to recognize the random dysfunctional boundaries defining and identifying a problem. When David sinned with Bathsheba, the injustice he had perpetrated was unclear to him until Nathan rebuked him in 2 Samuel 12:1-10. David was enraged when Samuel told him what someone had done. When Samuel informed David that he was the person who had committed the unjust deed, David was immediately sorrowful for his actions. Having a blind spot minimizes one's ability to perceive the non-ethical in themselves.

Nathan is significant in the story because he helps David see the impropriety and sin in his actions. Bazerman and Tenbrunsel (2011) recognized the difficulties associated with eliminating personal bias in decision-making and recommended having a trusted associate with whom you can bounce ideas and propose solutions. The challenge is that you must be willing to listen to and accept the input they provide. When Peter acted one way when he was alone with the Gentiles and another way when other Jewish church representatives showed up, Paul confronted him and challenged his hypocritical behavior (Galatians 2:11). It is essential to point out that Evans and Holman (2019) identified Paul's rebuke as an act of love – love for God, love for Peter, and love for those disenchanted by Peter's deceitful behavior. Again, love is God's catalyst for discipline, so His followers must recognize a need for accountability and then pursue it as a matter of God's love persuading them to act.

Another point of significance is David and Peter's willingness to submit to the inequity pointed out to them. Nathan and Paul act as advocates for the Holy Spirit to remind them of the righteous path they should be on and following. Once Nathan and Paul confront their friends, the friends can reject their warnings and continue to pursue ill-advised courses of action. God never intended for people to be alone, and having a godly accountability partner can "save your soul from death" (*ESV*, 2001/2016, James 5:20). There is mutual goodness in accountability in that adherence to God's Word would enable Timothy to promote the maturation of the Ephesian believers who in turn would take note of Timothy's commitment to the ministry (Evans & Holmon, 2019). Paul concluded that Timothy's diligent service would be a source of personal and corporate deliverance and transformation. Signs in airports encourage people to say something when they see it; the same is true in the Christian walk. When you see something amiss, you are responsible for initiating corrective measures, while the recipient of your accountability advances must assess, confess, and refocus their efforts. Both parties have a love requirement – to act in love and respond in love because today, it is someone else's blind spot, and tomorrow, it will be your blind spot that comes to light.

God's Word – The Standard

There has always been abundant published material with instructions and information for every activity under the sun. Solomon's confirmation of the endless quantity of books available, even during his lifetime, speaks volumes to the ever-increasing number of books, authors, influencers, and experts on every topic imaginable. The same is true of the writings related to God's Word, but God's unchanging Word alone serves as the penultimate source for standards for the godly character required of leaders of God's people. Scripture differs dramatically from America's Constitution in several ways, but as the Psalmist stated, "Forever, O Lord, Your Word is firmly fixed in the heavens" (*ESV*, 2001/2016, Psalm 119:89). No amendments or additions are required. His Word and His Word alone suffice as a "lamp to [our] feet and a light to [the] path" (*ESV*, 2001/2016, Psalm 119:105). So, what about God's Word elevates it over the numerous other sources of knowledge and wisdom in describing God's required character for leadership?

Well, the obvious answer is that if you are going to lead God's people,

God's Word must be the authoritative source for selection criteria. Recently, after winning a heavily disputed senatorial race in Georgia, the winning official, the Pastor of a historically relevant church, said, "It is my honor to utter the four most powerful words ever spoken in a democracy – The people have spoken." While not necessarily spoken in a democratic environment, others would argue the four most powerful words spoken anywhere are "Thus saith the Lord." When Paul emphasized the authority and usefulness of God's Word to Timothy, he did so by describing the Word's usefulness in a person's spiritual development, enabling them to be "complete, equipped for every good work" (*ESV*, 2001/2016, 2 Timothy 3:17). With that thought in mind, let us explore a few passages that highlight the priorities of God's Word spoken through Jesus Christ.

Trust in God – Faith (Luke 7:9)

Using the author of Hebrews to declare affirmatively that without faith, it was impossible to please God (Hebrews 11:6), God elevated the essential characteristic of faith to a place of prominence. Matthew and Luke recorded an instance of a Gentile Centurion who requested Jesus heal his servant and, by faith, realized that Jesus could heal an illness without being in the presence of the one who was sick. The Centurion's demonstration of faith, Bruehler (2022) contended, was more the miracle in this story than the healing of the servant and commented that the Centurion's faith was so rare that Luke's recording of this encounter did not end with words about Jesus or the Kingdom – the focus was on the extraordinary faith of a non-Jewish military man. Jesus was positively amazed by the Centurion's faith. However, He also could not believe the lack of faith of those in His hometown who experienced limited healing "because of their unbelief" (Mark 6:6). People demonstrating faith always moved Jesus. On one occasion, Luke described that presence as "the power of the Lord"

(*ESV*, 2001/2016, Luke 5:17) to heal the sick, and when His disciples doubted the impact of His presence and power, He labeled them as people of "little faith" (*ESV*, 2001/2016, Matthew 14:31; 16:8). By little, Jesus was referring to size and strength. Scott (2015) argued that Jesus proposed that if His followers had the faith of a mustard seed, they would do what would seem to be impossible in the natural world. Although the mustard seed was tiny, it was also powerful in that it produced a large plant; so, Jesus could be amazed at the miniature size of a person's faith while advocating for faith like a tiny mustard seed that produces the largest plant in the garden (Scott, 2015). God's Word sets men of strong and mighty faith as the standard for effective service.

Saying Yes to God – Self-Denial (Luke 9:23)

The common thought in the referenced account is that Jesus is addressing His disciples. Evans and Holman (2019) added the adjective "true" to differentiate between the fake and the following disciples (p. 979). Those truly following Him would have to say yes to following a future connected to Jesus's – one of suffering, slander, shame, and complete dependence on God (MacDonald, 1990). Jesus is speaking to a group identified in verse 18 as His disciples, yet there were among them those who had not fully committed to following Him. During a similar situation when there was a crowd of folks hanging around Him, Jesus laid out the high cost of being one of His disciples, then warned the pretenders to "count the cost" before seeking the position of the disciple (*ESV*, 2001/2016, Luke 14:25-33). A popular song by Shirley Caesar has as a part of its lyrics:

> "I'll say, 'Yes, Lord, yes,"
> To Your will and to Your way.
> I'll say, "Yes, Lord, yes,"
> I will trust you and obey.

When Your Spirit speaks to me,
With my whole heart, I'll agree:
And my answer will be, "Yes, Lord, yes!"

Leading God's people is about following God's Word – obedience and submission. Here is probably a good time to pause and consider – *Selah*. "Any one of you who does not renounce all that he has cannot be My disciple" (*ESV*, 2001/2016, Luke 14:33). Luke recorded it, but Jesus said it. According to God's Word, willingness to say no to me and yes to God is a non-negotiable option for Kingdom service.

Prioritizing God – Relationship (Luke 9:59-62)

This follower-to-leader thing is difficult. One must put complete trust and confidence in God, who expects that person to always say no to I and yes to the promptings of the Holy Spirit. The rough, bumpy road continues because a part of counting the cost is a re-ordering in the priority of my relationships. In the referenced pericope, Jesus invites three people to follow Him, and His invitations receive three unacceptable responses – an unwillingness to be homeless, burying a dead parent first, and saying goodbye to family. Some would say these are reasonable requests indicating a love and respect for their family. After all, before following Elijah, did not Elisha request to kiss his father and mother goodbye? Hays (2009) referred to Jesus's superiority to Elijah by noting that while it was all right to respond to Elijah, it was inappropriate for this individual to make the same request when Jesus invited him to discipleship. Jesus's response to these three prospects seemed to smack of disregard for family relations; however, Hays (2009) countered that Jesus was not disavowing or despising biological relationships but was prioritizing "the supreme call of following after Jesus" (p. 48). When Jesus advised the crowd following Him to count the cost before genuinely following Him, He used more pointed, direct verbiage demanding the hearers to consider their response. Jesus's requirement was for the would-be follower to hate his father, mother, wife, children, brothers, and sisters. Vine and Unger (1996) clarified the word translated into English as hate by noting the context denoted a preference for one thing over the other, requiring, in this instance, the choice of Jesus's claim on them over the claims of family members. That choice sometimes needs a Kingdom first mentality, but Hays (2009) added that there would not be physical or psychological hostility. As important as the family is in God's economy, God's Word demands prioritizing the leader's allegiance to their relationship with God over their natural, familial relationships. There is an old expression: God said it, I believe it, and that settles it. Whether one believes it or not, it is settled when God says it is. His Word calls for a faithful, obedient, and submissive leader committed to Christ's cause over the cause of kinship.

OBJECTIVES: LESSON TWO

To Compare Spiritual Growth with Departures from Spiritual Growth

Once upon a time, five people traveled from the same location to the same destination. As they traveled along the way, one of them experienced a terrible wreck; one of them jumped out of the vehicle while it was moving; one of them was on the designated path, driving the specified vehicle, but suddenly decided to switch vehicles; another chose an alternate destination; and the last person managed to negotiate the twists, turns, and tumults with their automobile intact. The people in this story were all "born of a woman" (*ESV*, 2001/2016, Job 14:1), but after their natural birth, they chose separate paths that Paul described for Timothy. The transporting vehicle is faith, and the first travelers "made shipwreck of their faith" (*ESV*, 2001/2016, 1 Timothy 1:19). Paul told the next travelers who jumped out of their moving vehicle as those who "will depart from the faith" (*ESV*, 2001/2016, 1 Timothy 4:1). As the third set of travelers were heading in the right direction, they got caught up in some senseless conversations then they "swerved from the faith" (*ESV*, 2001/2016, 1 Timothy 6:21). The last set of travelers stopped short of the targeted destination because they fell "in love with this present world" (*ESV*, 2001/2016, 2 Timothy 4:10). All believers have the biblical mandate to grow in their relationship with God; however, while growth is natural, it is not automatic.

1Timothy 1:19 – Shipwrecked the Faith

Here, Paul uses an example to which Timothy can relate. He names two Brothers in the faith, Hymenaeus and Alexander, who have wrecked their vehicle by not holding firm to faith and a good conscience. MacDonald (1990) compared them to sailors who have thrown their directional devices overboard and are navigating without an awareness of Spiritual guidance. Their destination is the rocks that will cause their destruction. We understand these men were Christians whom Paul had requested disciplinary measures so that God would restore them to the right relationship with Himself (Verbrugge, 1980). At this stage, a part of church discipline was separation from the body so that those making shipwrecks of their faith would not hinder the Spiritual growth of others (Verbrugge, 1980). Paul noted in 2 Corinthians 13:11 that the ultimate goal of discipline is restoration to fellowship and to service; however, the church leaders are to hand "over to Satan" those who resist restoration efforts.

1 Timothy 4:1 – Departed from (Spurned) the Faith

Scripture is replete with examples of fake believers who appear righteous but are self-righteous and will get out of the vehicle. MacDonald (1990) characterized them as people who demonstrate reformation without regeneration – people who pretend to be religious but have ulterior motives. These apostate people use godliness for gain, whether it be monetary or popularity. Jesus warned of the wolves in sheep's clothing who perform incredible feats but do not have a relationship with God (Matthew 7:15-23). Paul described them as people who have "the appearance of godliness but deny its power" (*ESV*, 2001/2016, 2 Timothy 3:5). As a leader of God's people, you will have to be discerning of those who seem to be with your group but are there to destroy the members because they are not genuine members. These wolves have an impact, and Paul would later describe those who cling to the false teaching as having "itching ears" and desiring to hear those things that are pleasing versus true things (*ESV*, 2001/2016, 2 Timothy 4:3). As a leader, you must remember that even when a wolf puts on the skin of a sheep, the wolf is still a wolf and desires to devour the sheep.

1 Timothy 6:21; 2 Timothy 2:17-18 – Swerved from the Faith

The devil is a liar, and Jesus called him "the father of lies" (*ESV*, 2001/2016, John 8:44). He lied to Eve and has been deceiving people ever since. After a person is born, Satan's job is to steal, kill, and destroy anything and anyone who would lead that person to a saving knowledge of Christ. Satan is also at work deceiving members of the body of Christ, and he likes nothing better than inserting the foolishness of "irreverent babble and contradictions" (*ESV*, 2001/2016, 1 Timothy 6:20) into the conversation and congregation of God's people. Vine and Unger (1996) categorized irreverent talk as antagonistic words against what is holy or divine. With that understanding, it is clearer why Hymenaeus' faith would be heading towards shipwreck. He and Philetus had attached themselves to the foolish, unholy teachings of those who falsely peddled them under the guise of passing on knowledge. Paul warned Timothy about getting involved in back-and-forth conversations with these purveyors of false knowledge because he saw how it affected believing Brothers like Hymenaeus and Philetus (2 Timothy 2:16-17). As God's representative, you should not get into tit for tat; however, you cannot allow opponents of the truths of God's Word to go unchallenged. Peter's advice provided the guidance needed to counter unholy talk while defending the source of your hope – you must present your conversation with "gentleness and respect" (*ESV*, 2001/2016, 1 Peter 3:15). Elsewhere, Paul instructed your speech to be seasoned with salt (Colossians 4:6). Those who are swerving away from the faith must be gently and graciously confronted with toned down rhetoric (Galatians 6:1). As leaders, you have the dual challenge of avoiding foolish talk that portends swerving while being prepared to rescue the swervers – and using the therapeutic measures of discipline as needed.

2 Timothy 4:10 – Substituted Faith

Our referenced verse highlights those who have served faithfully in the vineyard but become enamored with the world and terminate their enlistment. Demas, a former co-worker with Paul whom Paul mentioned in his letters to the Colossians (4:14) and Philemon (v. 24), deserted him in favor of worldly pursuits. Some of you may fall away because you do not have the resolve, like Moses, to resist "the fleeting pleasures of sin" (*ESV*, 2001/2016, Hebrews 11:25), resorting instead, like Demas, to worldly desires. Evans and Holman (2019) summed up the folly of Demas's decision by describing it as a selection of the earthly and a rejection of that which is eternal. Using a different perspective, Walker (2012) posited that the Colossians verse referred to a time after Paul wrote 2 Timothy. This indicates that Demas returned to working with Paul after backsliding – choosing not to serve with Paul. MacDonald (1990) also speculated that

Demas may have deserted Paul to avoid suffering the persecution Paul was experiencing. Regardless of the timeline, there was a period of Demas's life when he substituted faith in God for the folly of the world. When, and if, the love of the world or things in the world occurs, God offers forgiveness, cleansing, and restoration to fellowship to those who will confess their disobedience. There is evidence of this type of Spiritual growth after a demonstration of immaturity in 2 Timothy. Paul requested Timothy to bring John Mark with him when he visited him in Rome – the same John Mark who had deserted Paul and Barnabas (Acts 13:13) and was the person at the center of the breakup between Paul and Barnabas (Acts 15:37-40). With the passing of time and John Mark's Spiritual growth and development, Paul recognized that this Brother who had departed from Spiritual growth had now returned to the vehicle of faith in God and would be of excellent service to Paul during his remaining time in ministry (2 Timothy 4:11). So, whether you have made shipwreck of your faith, spurned the faith, swerved from, or substituted for faith, God stands ready to receive you back in His good graces because His Son "always lives to make intercession for them" (*ESV*, 2001/2016, Hebrews 7:25).

To Acknowledge Areas for Growth and Development

When you do not know where you are going, any road will take you there. So, to avoid putting the character cart before the workhorse, we must identify areas for growth and development and acknowledge their validity. Earlier, we determined through Zaccaro et al. (2000) that leaders generally do not go beyond information familiar to them and consider unique solutions because those solutions resided in the leader's blind spots. Some of your shortcomings may be obvious, while others are inconspicuous and require external identification to differentiate between who you think you are and who you are. In Paul's writings to Timothy, he modeled an admission of what he was and expressed how God could use his weakness for His glory.

After we look briefly at Paul's admission to Timothy, there are some areas in Timothy's life Paul implies may need strengthening. If we get beyond ourselves, we mentioned using God's Word as the standard – it is a lamp revealing the next steps for travel (Psalm 119:105). Believers have access to the Holy Spirit, who searches all things and can reveal the hidden areas of our hearts requiring cleansing (Psalm 139:23-24). There is Scripture, we have the Holy Spirit, and Solomon advised listening carefully to those who are genuinely friends because their words are trustworthy (Proverbs 27:5-6). Finally, there is self-examination that we must conduct to determine how well we are living in line with the Scripture, the Spirit, and our supporters (1 Corinthians 11:28-34). When leaders do not avail themselves of these avenues, they can become victims and then victimize their followers by their inability and unwillingness to acknowledge areas for growth and development.

Paul's Admission

Many people fall into the category of those who act like they have been saved all their lives. They have a holier-than-thou attitude and refuse to be gracious, merciful, and forgiving of those who have fallen short of God's glory like them. Paul did not fit into that category because he often retold the story of his life before Christ but not for self-glorification –as proof of God's goodness and His willingness to reach as deep as needed to save sinners. Although Timothy had traveled and ministered extensively with Paul, Paul felt the need to reinforce the mercy he received from God (1 Timothy 1:13, 16). Maybe Paul wanted Timothy to know that God's mercy was available to him as a catalyst for his maturing. Brueggemann

(1992) described God's mercy as "an intrusive force who reshapes all of reality for the sake of joy, well-being, and life" (p. 741). Paul needed a forceful redirection of his life because, in his ignorance and unbelief, he was the primary persecutor of the church (1 Timothy 1:12-16). With his background, God had to appoint Paul to His service because no church member would have believed his conversion. So, Paul repeatedly reminded Timothy of his divine appointment to emphasize God's grace and mercy and to explain that God calls whom He will and uses them as He determines. Paul's recognition of God's work and willingness to testify of that work gave him clarity. It served as a caution, reminding him of his need for self-examination, attentiveness to the Holy Spirit, and the necessity of studying God's Word.

As Paul's companion and his "true child in the faith" (*ESV*, 2001/2016, 1 Timothy 1:2), Timothy and Paul would qualify as friends – friends who are friends indeed, willing to wound in the short term to ensure wellness in the long term. As we read through Paul's letters to Timothy, here are some characteristics Paul mentions to Timothy that leaders would do well to allow Scripture, the Spirit, and their supporters to guide their self-examination.

Avoiding Foolish Talk

Multiple times in Paul's writings to Timothy, he cautions Timothy of the dangers associated with misusing words. A rhyme from years ago made light of words used derogatorily: "Sticks and stones can break my bones, but names will never hurt break me" (Bard, 1962, p. 158). Although the intent of this adage may be to downplay the impact of words used carelessly when communicating with another person, the truth is that words misused, imprecisely, and incorrectly can break a person's spirit. When the false teachers in Ephesus used words to mislead the people,

Campbell (1997) declared that Paul used words to describe their teaching as idle chatter, gossip, and stories that only older women would care about. Timothy was to avoid these distractions and these detractors from his mission. MacDonald (1990) posited that although Timothy, as a church leader, was not to be argumentative with the false teachers, he still had the responsibility to contend for the truth; however, his objective and methodology should point to instruction rather than winning an argument. Peter agreed with Paul and noted that the defenders of the true gospel must do so "with gentleness and respect" (*ESV*, 2001/2016, 1 Peter 3:15). What a challenge you are taking on as a prospective leader – How does one contend without becoming contentious? A song I learned as a child comes to mind, "Oh be careful little mouth what you say…For the Father up above is looking down with tender love. Oh, be careful little mouth what you say." Our examination focuses on the aim Paul presented to Timothy – love from a pure heart, a clear conscience, and sincere faith (1 Timothy 1:5). Go and do thou likewise!

Courage in Challenging Circumstances

Indications are that Timothy was not only young but also shy and timid. Lawson's (2002) research determined that Timothy was young, going into a church that had not requested his presence, and had several wealthy congregants prepared to pounce on a Timid Timothy. So, Timothy would need the Holy Spirit to experience the enhanced and empowered enablement for public proclamation. As the leading elder in the Ephesian church, Timothy would have to guide everyone in that fellowship, so Paul encouraged Timothy to speak boldly about life and doctrine. Paul wanted Timothy to imitate Jesus and emulate Him. When Matthew described how Jesus taught, he said that Jesus differed from the other teachers because he spoke with authority (Matthew 7:29). When Jesus spoke, He exercised discernment, knowing when to be silent and not answer (Luke 23:9) but also when and how to silence His critics (Matthew 22:21-22). Pao (2014) reasoned that Timothy's age would make carrying out his role and responsibilities within the more chronologically advanced Ephesian church challenging. Hence, Paul pronounced a double imperative – one for Timothy to not allow anyone to intimidate him because of his youth and two for the church to accept Timothy's position as one conferred upon him by Paul's apostolic authority (Pao, 2014). With Timothy assuming the leadership role, Evans and Holman (2019) offered that his life, in word and deed, must be in synch so that he modeled the truths he was verbalizing. Furthermore, since fear is not from God, every time Timothy faced a potentially fearful situation, he could claim as David did, "When I am afraid, I put my trust in You" (*ESV*, 2001/2016, Psalm 56:3). There will come times when you, acting on your strength and wisdom, will be fearful, intimidated, and mindful of your relative chronological existence. At those times, you must lean on your supporters as they point you to the Spirit by referencing Scripture.

MODULE TWO – LESSON THREE

DEVELOPING THE GODLY QUALITY OF MY CHARACTER

OVERVIEW

- The leader's practice must match the leader's preaching.
- Leaders get better by persistently practicing the principles of God's Word.
- The Spiritual development of the leader is an ongoing activity.

LESSON OBJECTIVES

- To allow the Holy Spirit to guide in Spiritual growth and development.
- To anticipate the benefits of perseverance through challenging times.

SCRIPTURE READINGS

- 1 Timothy 1:12, 4:6, 5:1-2, 6:8, 11
- 2 Timothy 1:4, 7, 2:2, 10, 17, 25, 3:12, 4:7, 11, 16

Key Words

Servant	Joy
Teacher	Forgiveness

OVERVIEW

Practice Must Match Preaching

The other day, I was involved in a discussion with a group of gentlemen – one of them was very upset about what he perceived as hypocrisy from his pastor. He gave example after example of behaviors the pastor engaged in Monday through Saturday that were at odds with the messages he delivered on Sunday. Inconsistency between practice and preaching is not a new phenomenon. It is one Jesus warned His followers to avoid (Matthew 23:3). Evans and Holman (2019) labeled their behavior as hypocritical, while MacDonald (1990) resorted to more colorful language – he called it "a case of high talk and low walk" (p. 104). One sure way to minimize your effectiveness in leadership is to put demands on your followers that you have no intention or capability of living out in your life. Paul wanted to ensure that was not the case with Timothy, so he insisted that Timothy persistently practice the principles of God's Word that he was preaching.

An old saying states that practice makes perfect; some have modified that statement to say that perfect practice makes perfect. Either way, Paul wanted Timothy to publicly put into practice the habits he was preparing in private. Dionson (2015) compared Paul's encouragement to practice to a coach prodding a protégé to commit to doing everything needed to become fully immersed and committed to excellence. As the leader, Timothy would be on display, modeling for the church the behaviors they should emulate (1 Timothy 3:15; 4:12). The only way to get better at an activity is the repetitive practice of that activity in varying environments comparable to the locus of praxis.

People in the sports world remember a well-known sports figure going on a rant about practicing and how this star devalued the importance of practicing – especially considering performing in a game. Not only did this athlete diminish the importance of practice on an individual level, but the athlete also ignored the collective team's advantage of preparation. Williams and Hodges (2005) went to great lengths to describe the value practicing has on achieving excellence. Their research revealed that while there was some benefit in being naturally "gifted," those who practiced more were significantly more likely to attain elite status than those not given to the habit of practicing (Williams & Hodges, 2005, p. 638). Centuries earlier, Paul understood this principle of action and called on Timothy to be about the business of practicing. Considering Timothy's role in the Ephesian church, Lawson (2002) posited that practicing reading, exhortation, and teaching would enable Timothy and his hearers to accurately apply the Word based on the deliberate delivery of doctrine.

PRACTICE PERSISTENTLY THE PRINCIPLES OF GOD'S WORD

Paul intentionally gave Timothy a model for clearly presenting God's Word. Paul's regimen would require devotion to public Scripture reading, exhortation, and teaching. Lawson (2002) surmised that these three were imperatives for Timothy to preach from the Word of God by providing the people with relevant applications founded on sound doctrine. Timothy's practice of "these things" was an exercise in using his giftedness. Grudem (2014) conjectured that with constant, consistent, committed use, Timothy's Spiritual competency would increase in strength and effectiveness. The last of "these things" required Timothy to prepare to preach the Word, to live out the dictates of the Word, and to hold others accountable for the truths of the Word.

Timothy had been with Paul when Paul revealed to those traveling with him that the Holy Spirit made it clear to him that every city he visited would either put him in prison or assault him physically and mentally (Acts 20:23). Yet Timothy witnessed that Paul continued ministering from city to city. Because Timothy was a student of the Word, he understood from James's writing that trying a person's faith produces commitment that would enable the tested person to mature in their relationship with God (James 1:3-4). Finally, Timothy had Jesus's example as He moved intentionally and purposefully to Jerusalem, not allowing anything or anyone to deter Him from accomplishing what His Father had given Him to do. God convinced Paul that He had begun a good work in him and would continue that work, by way of succession, until the day of Jesus's return (Philippians 1:6). Paul's insistence on perseverance highlighted the need to train young Timothy who would be able to select and teach others who would then train others also. The recruitment or acceptance of aspirants should not be initiated when a vacancy occurs but should be a continuous process to build and develop a talent pool (Rothwell, 2010). Encouraging and modeling persistence are major contributing factors to the success of any succession planning endeavor.

Leader Growth and Development is an Ongoing Process

FMIFC is a process designed to prepare young people for positions of leadership. Since young people become older, this process requires a quality control entry measure. Paul's directive to Timothy to ensure qualitative succession was that Timothy pass on what he learned and was learning "to faithful men who will be able to teach others also" (*ESV*, 2001/2016,

2 Timothy 2:2). Continual use of this model would be essential for the ongoing effectiveness of the Ephesian church. Without deviating from Paul's quality control entry measure, there are branches and sequels you need to be aware that FMIFC incorporates with you as learners that leaders must continually review and implement. Rothwell (2010) described several approaches to organizational succession that we can see possibly implemented in the Ephesian church.

Moving people into an organization

This approach involves bringing in a person who is not affiliated with the organization to lead the group. For Rothwell (2010), this approach is the riskiest because it is a complete gamble about the level of effectiveness the person will achieve with the existing people accustomed to working under existing values and beliefs. Most of the time, when bringing a person in from the outside, there is a lack of familiarity with the person's track record and their ability and willingness to adjust (Rothwell, 2010). Paul's selection of Timothy avoided his uncertainty about the candidate; however, it did not eliminate the church's uncertainty about Timothy or erase his personality and disposition (Lawson, 2002). Ultimately, the decision was to move Timothy into the Ephesian church as its leader.

Moving people out of an organization

As we have seen, many teachers in the church were confidently making assertions that some in the congregation accepted (1 Timothy 1:7). When selection of a new leader requires moving people out of the organization, there will be firings, people laid off, downsizing, and other personnel actions that have negative implications (Rothwell, 2010). In this example, the new leader, Timothy, would face the challenge of removing the ineffective, disingenuous teachers/leaders from their places of influence (1 Timothy 1:3-4). Although succession through removal can be complicated, Rothwell (2010) also ventured into the possibility of openings resulting from the removals.

Moving people up in an organization

Using this technique involves knowledge that people within the organization are qualified to assume positions of increased responsibility and authority. Rothwell (2010) wrote of the positives using this model (upward mobility, advancement, sustained philosophies, and cultures) and cautioned of the drawbacks – primarily selecting a person from within with exemplary job performance in one position who is not able to achieve the same level of competence at the next level. As Jason Fried famously stated, "Past performance is not a guarantee of future results." However, Paul provided Timothy and Christian churches guidance for promotion within – elders and deacons. Paul noted the necessity of testing candidates before assigning them to leadership positions (1 Timothy 3:10), and MacDonald (1990) suggested a proving ground may be to have candidates for leadership assume relatively minor roles in the church to allow them to demonstrate their potential for greater responsibilities and authority.

Talent and Acceleration Pools

Although these approaches are separate means of accomplishing the emplacement of future leaders, both succession methodologies have elements germane to the account in Paul's writings to Timothy. Taylor and Bennett (2002) detailed a procedure for identifying and developing a pool of qualified (talented) candidates to choose and sort using established criteria. The candidates chosen had the opportunity to participate in developmental programs in preparation for potential selection for leadership. There was probably a group of leadership aspirants in Ephesus who would be selected, like those moving up in an organization, and tested to determine the likelihood of their effectiveness as an elder or deacon.

Like the talent pool, the acceleration pool identifies, develops, and promotes high achievers within an organization (Taylor & Bennett, 2002). A distinction Rothwell (2010) made is that acceleration pools are more common in eminent succession needs of an entity with several aged leaders likely leaving the workforce simultaneously. As the accelerated pool name suggests, identifying, developing, and promoting leaders is accelerated to meet the organization's needs. In the Ephesus example, Paul had already selected Timothy as the leader; however, Timothy had to be aware of his need to teach and model godliness to demonstrate his competence, values, and ethics.

OBJECTIVES: LESSON THREE

TO ALLOW THE HOLY SPIRIT TO GUIDE IN SPIRITUAL GROWTH AND DEVELOPMENT

God's Word calls out the Christian's inability to do work worthy of God's recognition as gold, silver, or precious stones without Spiritual assistance. Jesus said the Holy Spirit, though, would guide the believers "into all truth" (*ESV*, 2001/2016, John 16:13), empowering those believers to accomplish all God's intentions for them through them. As we look at Paul's words to Timothy, there are several character development areas listed for Timothy. As learners and leaders, we would do well to allow the Holy Spirit to do His formation work in our lives. We will delve into His work in our lives to develop confidence, understand His control, appreciate His comfort, and heed His cautions. Fortunately, or unfortunately, depending on your perspective, God will not force these capabilities on you. As my Dad used to say, "God is a Gentleman; He will not force you to do anything." However, our effectiveness as leaders is contingent upon our submission as followers.

2 Timothy 1:7 – Confidence

Like many people stepping out of the shadows into the spotlight, Timothy was reluctant to expose himself to external, exacting examination challenges. Moses claimed he had a speech impediment (Exodus 4:10); Amos was unsure of his hereditary qualifications (Amos 7:14); and Mary questioned God's ability to make her a mother while she remained a virgin (Luke 1:34). Evans and Holman (2019) speculated that Timothy had some doubts about his abilities to lead because of his timidity, fearfulness, and maybe the lack of having strong male role models in his youth. The Holy Spirit would provide the resources of power, love, and sound judgment for Timothy to be effective in his leadership capacity. Once again, your effectiveness as a godly leader will not come from your magnetic personality or highly developed intelligence. Your competence and sufficiency will reflect your submission to the work of the Holy Spirit in your life.

It was fear that dominated a young, timid, and inexperienced Timothy. Paul wrote that fear is not a gift of the Holy Spirit. Instead, as Kleinig (2017) pointed out, the Holy Spirit empowered Timothy with "the power to love in a sound-minded way" (p. 8) that would empower Timothy to be resilient in the face of challenges within and without while demonstrating love for the detractors in a manner that was free of emotional and spiritual abuse. Regardless of the circumstances he faced, Timothy would have the discretion not to act rashly, foolishly, or out of line with the Holy Spirit's gift of self-control (MacDonald, 1990). When you face the confrontations presented to you, despite your youth, personality, and minimal experience, you can rest assured the Holy Spirit can still produce power, love, and self-control in you as you yield to Him. As David discovered, when fear assailed him, he took those opportunities to trust in God (Psalm 56:3). Whenever fear arises in carrying out your God-assigned tasks, you can always yield your will to His way and utilize the power, love, and sound mindedness He provides.

2 Timothy 1:14 – Control

Sporting events take place in and on surfaces with lines that contain the activity taking place on them. Inappropriately crossing those lines results in a penalty, and at other times, when the athletes exceed the boundaries, they receive a reward for their achievements. From the beginning, God established limits for physical activities, which remain in place. The sun only rules the day (Genesis 1:16), the ocean can only go so far (Job 38:8-11), and man could eat from every tree in the garden but one (Genesis 2:16-17). Regarding God's Word, He made it clear that there were not to be any additions or deletions (Deuteronomy 4:2). With all the ungodly influences in Ephesus, Timothy would need the indwelling Holy Spirit's enablement for him to hold on to the teachings from God's Word that he had heard Paul proclaim and witnessed him living out.

The city of Ephesus had many teachers who were perverting God's Word. As Paul informed Timothy, many of them had infiltrated the Ephesian households of women within the church. They were leading them and others astray because they had a form of godliness. However, their teachings lacked a demonstration of God's power. As a result, the people had increased knowledge and information but a corresponding deficit in truth (2 Timothy 3:6-7). The meetings looked like and sounded like church. Still, the content was out of control – the teachers were straying away from God's Word and substituting various ascetic practices that sounded religious because of their rigid requirements while denying God as the provider of the relationship, food, and the days. Evans and Holman (2019) posited Paul's encouragement to Timothy to protect the gospel by faithfully speaking truth to those who would step outside the boundaries of God's Word. For Timothy to guard the truth, Paul told him he would have to rely on the Holy Spirit because he could not use his strength against the forces of wickedness (MacDonald, 1990).

As you continue in your learning leadership walk with God, your attentiveness and obedience to the words of Scripture, which the Holy Spirit generates in you, will make your paths straight. Kleinig (2017) compared the godly guided use of Scripture to a doctor providing medication and treatments that will heal the body and soul and contrasted it with words used carelessly that can hamper healing. When the Holy Spirit controls the words, there is a clear delineation between the law and the gospel and a dependency on Him to preserve its healing efficacy (Kleinig, 2017). As you use words to promote the growth of God's people, you must stay between the lines of His Word and under the guidance of His Holy Spirit.

2 Timothy 4:22 – Comfort

As Paul completed his earthly ministry, he passed Timothy the encouraging reassurance and reminder of the Spirit's presence always being available to provide comfort regardless of whatever turmoil may be occurring around him. When writing to the Corinthian church, Paul detailed the Spirit of God communicating with man's spirit "so that we might understand the things freely given us by God" (*ESV*, 2001/2016, 1 Corinthians 2:12). As our comforter and helper, the Holy Spirit is God's agent of comfort. The early church experienced the comfort of the Holy Spirit as He built them up (Acts 9:31). Similarly, the believers in Philippi received comfort and encouragement as they interacted with the Spirit (Philippians 2:1). Your interactions with the Holy Spirit should cause you to imitate the

Father who is the source of comfort and through His Holy Spirit has enabled believers to be agents of His comfort (2 Corinthians 1:3-4). In his conclusion to Timothy, Paul addressed Timothy and all the Ephesian saints with him as an indication of the Spirit of comfort that must exist within the body. The churches refreshed Paul in his many persecutions, so we ought to provide comfort like that we have fittingly received or would desire to receive (Vine & Unger, 1976). We have the injunction to use words as a source of comfort – words guided and provided by the Spirit.

1 Timothy 4:1 – Caution

When people are confident, in control, and living in their comfort zone, they tend to throw caution to the wind. As believers, the level of confidence, control, and comfort we experience derives from our attentiveness and obedience to the Holy Spirit. However, some of your growth and development requires caution – caution, not fear. Remember, fear is not a fruit of the Holy Spirit but a deterrent from exercising your power, love, and sound-mindedness. In the referenced verse, Paul told Timothy of a warning given to him by the Holy Spirit, cautioning him to be aware of those who would make it their business to deceive others with false, heretical teaching. Because Paul phrased the warning as he did, Campbell (1997) surmised that Paul was writing prophetically based on a communication directly from the Holy Spirit about heretical events happening while Paul was writing and would also occur in the future. Paul was aware of the warnings from the Holy Spirit. The Holy Spirit warned Paul about the impending dangers awaiting him in the cities he would travel to (Acts 20:36). Paul received the warning and was not surprised when the imprisonments and troubles occurred.

The caution generated by Paul's warning has as much relevance now as when he wrote it. MacDonald (1990) speculated that the quantity of "some" in 1 Timothy would increase dramatically in 2 Timothy and would be exponentially larger now with the proliferation of cults (p. 907). Those deceiving and being deceived were earthly victims of the spiritual warfare going on "in heavenly places" (*ESV*, 2001/2016, Ephesians 6:12), leading to departures from the faith, lying, and an inability to distinguish truth from error (Evans & Holman, 2019). The purveyors of the apostasies, Campbell (1997) stated, were under demonic influence, were hypocrites, and were victims of an inability to differentiate between the religion of asceticism and the righteousness of association with Christ through the Holy Spirit. So, you should not be surprised when people seem to be with you but are there to destroy the fellowship. Jesus called them wolves masquerading as sheep (Matthew 7:15). People will follow the false teachers because the people can relate to their form of godliness without submitting to the lordship of Jesus Christ. Learners, this is your message of caution. We deliver it now; however, the Holy Spirit will guide you as you listen.

God is the Source of Understanding and Senses – 2 Timothy 2:7, 26

As my son was growing up, his favorite verse was Proverbs 4:7 (*New International Version*, 1978/1984), "Wisdom is supreme; therefore get wisdom. Though it cost all you have, get understanding." Solomon elevated the acquisition of understanding to the highest level and underscored the value of Issachar's sons, who understood the times in which they were living and applied their understanding in guiding their fellow citizens to take suitable courses of action (1 Chronicles 12:32). Knowing without wisdom, Paul posited, leads to pride (1 Corinthians 8:1) yet having wisdom without godly understanding makes one susceptible to attempting to understand with the natural mind things requiring spiritual discernment (1 Corinthians 2:14). What form would the understanding God gives take when He gives it to Timothy or us?

Some have posited a supernatural transfer of words and wisdom that would give the speaker inexplicable abilities. A likely source of this thought process would be Jesus's instructions to His disciples when the religious leaders would press them to make a statement in defense of their beliefs. They would not need to prepare a statement because "the Holy Spirit will teach you in that very hour what you ought to say" (*ESV*, 2001/2016, Luke 12:12). Arp (2012) argued that enablement was only and expressly for Jesus's disciples and not applicable to others. When Arp (2012) wrote of the understanding the Lord would give Timothy, he defined understanding as intellectual comprehension of something that challenges how people think or conduct their lives. After giving Timothy examples of a soldier, an athlete, and a farmer, Paul instructed Timothy to think (spend some time in contemplation) over the implications of those examples. By going deeper than the surface level, Timothy could make a considered application to the challenges of Christian life. MacDonald (1990) added that when Timothy meditated on the examples, he would be able to correlate the responsibilities of ministry with the rewards of ministry. Later in the second chapter, Paul would again instruct Timothy to meditate so that he would be able to rightly apply the truths of Scripture (2 Timothy 2:15). The benefit of understanding would come from the Holy Spirit; however, Timothy would still need to develop the habit of studying so that he could access the insightful discernment provided by the Holy Spirit.

The other side of understanding is people's actions when they realize they have strayed from the path. God can cause these people to, as Paul told Timothy, "come to their senses" (*ESV*, 2001/2016, 2 Timothy 2:26). Vine and Unger (1996) described these words as a return to sobriety from an altered state of consciousness. When the prodigal son realized his sinful behavior towards his father, Luke said, "he came to himself" (*ESV*, 2001/2016, Luke 15:17). MacDonald (1990) noted that the prodigal did not come to that conclusion before thinking and remembering. When translated into English, Luke used the exact words to describe Peter's level of awareness when God rescued him from Herod and imprisonment. Coming to one's senses is a return to sanity and safety. When Peter left the prison, he was in a daze, but as he recognized reality, he recalled where he was and how to get to the house where the people were praying for him. As Timothy studied to understand and endured the trials around him without giving in to foolish conversations and arguing, he could present the truths of God's Word in a relevant way. God will use the teaching to bring wayward, wandering prodigals to their senses.

My mom used to say, "You cannot come back from someplace you have never been." For those impacted by the waywardness of sin, the path back is through confession and repentance. These folks were adequately related to God at one point, but something or someone lured them away. As Evans and Holman (2019) reminded those attempting to assist those coming back, kindness and patient gentleness are the keys to correcting the course of the wanderer. As a leader, you must avoid getting involved in foolish conversations that lead to arguments and not repentance. You cannot allow the opponents of truth to go unchallenged; however, you must present your defense of the gospel that will bring the drifter back with "gentleness and respect" (*ESV*, 2001/2016, 1 Peter 3:15). Remember, it is God's kindness that leads wanderers to come to their senses; so, to be more like Him, you will have to tone down your rhetoric.

MODULE 3

THE CHALLENGES OF LEADERSHIP

MODULE INTRODUCTION

Welcome to the third module of the FMIFC curriculum process. In this module, we will be covering the Challenges of Leadership. This module will again focus on Paul's writings to Timothy and the challenges he faced as a young leader that other young godly leaders may confront. There will always be challenges for those who would be leaders. Sometimes, the challenges come as situations, while people are the source of conflict at other times. As a leader of God's church, you must realize that God allowed it, so the difficulty is for your development and God's glory. We will begin by attempting to understand why leaders face challenges, move on to the source of those challenges, and conclude with some strategies for overcoming the complexities of leadership. Below is an overview of the content we will cover during this segment.

Module Three Overview

	Lesson One: Why Leaders Face Challenges	**Lesson Two:** Challenges: Who and What	**Lesson Three:** Overcoming the Complexities of Leadership.
Overview:	* In this world, you will have tribulation. * A servant is not greater than the master. * Jannes and Jambres opposed Moses.	* What makes people a challenge? * What makes situations challenging? * How does God use challenges to develop His leaders?	* To be forewarned is to be forearmed. * Learning from our examples, i.e., Jesus and Paul.
Objectives:	* To prepare for opposition. * To view opposition as developmental opportunities.	* To contend without becoming contentious. * To recognize and rectify relationships over religion. * To uncover the benefits of grace and mercy.	* To urge and request prayer. * To diligently study and practice. * To understand that you are a person serving in a leadership position with a specific purpose. .
Scripture Readings:	1 Timothy 1:3-11, 2:8, 4:1-5, 12, 2 Timothy 3:1-9, 4:9-18	1 Timothy 1:3-11, 2:9-15, 4:1-5, 12, 6: 1-10, 2 Timothy 2:23-25, 3:1-9	1 Timothy 3:1-13, 4:12-16, 6:1-10, 20, 2 Timothy 1:6, 13-14, 2:1-7, 3:14, 4:5
Vocabulary/Key Words:	Abstinence, purity, stewardship, unappeasable	Speculation, dissension, depraved	Doctrine, bondservants, content

MODULE THREE – LESSON ONE

WHY LEADERS FACE CHALLENGES

Overview

- In this world, you will have tribulation.
- A servant is not greater than the master.
- Jannes and Jambres opposed Moses.

Lesson Objectives

- To prepare for opposition.
- To view challenges as developmental.
- To model God for those observing.

Scripture Readings

- 1 Timothy 1:3-11, 2:8, 4:1-5, 12,
- 2 Timothy 3:1-9, 4:9-18

KEY WORDS

Abstinence	Purity
Stewardship	Unappeasable

OVERVIEW

In sports, a home-field advantage affords the hosting team a competitive edge because they are familiar with the facility, the folks, and the footing. For the Christian, Scripture describes the world as a temporary dwelling place because "our citizenship is in heaven" (*ESV*, 2001/2016, Philippians 3:20). While you remain in the world and maintain your love for God over the things in this world, you will have tribulation (John 16:33). Jesus, as our Master and model, faced challenges of every sort then warned His followers that it would not be different for them because servants are not more significant than their masters (John 15:20). They should not expect folks on the other team to treat them well. Watch out for them because they can cause massive disruptions to the work God has called you to do (2 Timothy 4: 15). Unfortunately, there is also a need to be situationally aware of the surroundings, the footing, because we have teammates like Jannes and Jambres (2 Timothy 3:8) who are working against us. There will be challenges along Leadership Avenue; however, you must view those challenges as opportunities to excel and be an example for those looking to you for leadership.

OBJECTIVES: LESSON ONE

TO PREPARE FOR OPPOSITION – 1 TIMOTHY 1:3-11

"Forewarned is forearmed" is an old proverb describing that when one receives a warning of a particular situation, one should take precautionary measures to avoid the potential dangers of that situation. As Paul began his letter to Timothy, he provided some information to make him aware of his work environment and challenge him to reside in Ephesus – a city besieged with perverted teachers. Many describe the books of Timothy and Titus as pastoral letters; however, MacDonald (1990) posited the idea of Timothy being on a "temporary mission" with some tasks to complete and some doctrinal information to dispense (p. 891). Conversely, Evans and Holman (2019) described this letter as Paul's guidance to Timothy to continue the work that he had started in Ephesus. Timothy needed to know what he was up against, whether the work was temporary or long-term. Paul also informs Timothy of the other team's plays and gives current-day readers guidance and warnings (a scouting report).

Vain Words – 1 Timothy1:4, 6, 6:20

Words are a primary tool of the opposing team. The serpent questioned God's directive to His creation (Genesis 3:1), and the devil used words to tempt Jesus (Matthew 4:1-9). In Ephesus, false teachers used myths and genealogies to distort God's creative order by stirring up dangerous, controversial conversations within the church (Bond, 2006). Paul argued that the verbal exchanges were pointless and meaningless because they drew attention away from God's Word and created what Heringer (2021) described as heterodoxy – teaching contrary to the doctrine Paul taught and preached. Catt (2013) expanded on this description, called it heresy (mixing truth with error), and stated Timothy's job was to condemn heresy and not to accept or compromise with it. Some portion of the Ephesian church had swerved into this perversion – some were teaching it, and others were believing it, with both leaving the path of orthodoxy.

God may call you to a situation where believers are swerving from the truth. MacDonald (1990) speculated that Timothy may have thought about leaving Ephesus because of his personality, but Paul commanded him to stay there. Once God points you to your assigned place of ministry, you may consider the temptation to leave the situation or place where God has planted you. God has a mission for you to accomplish there, and as His mouthpiece, you will have the privilege of using words to counter the words of distraction with the message of accountability to God. You know it is coming, so stay focused.

Legal Misapplications – 1 Timothy 1:7-11

The other day, as some associates and I were discussing faith, one of them pointed emphatically to the Word, which proclaimed hearing as the source of faith. Well, the Word goes on to specify that faith in God comes from hearing God's Word (Romans 10:17). One of the primary means of instruction is by verbalizing words, and in Ephesus, some teachers were verbalizing teachings about the Mosaic Law. The problem Paul warned Timothy about was that the instruction was coming from teachers who had no familiarity with the law; they were making their assertions confidently, which resulted in the diversion of members of the church to paths "contrary to sound doctrine" (*ESV*, 2001/2016, 1 Timothy 1:10). Paul was warning Timothy of the play the opposing team used so that he could effectively counter it.

Timothy, that is all the leaders and learners, your place of servant-leadership will include those who have relegated themselves to living in the past. They are committed to a continuation of or a return to the way they have traditionally accomplished a task. Traditions, like the law, are only beneficial "if one uses them lawfully" (*ESV*, 2001/2016, 1 Timothy 1:8). There must be a differentiation between "the tradition of men" and the "commandment of God" (*ESV*, 2001/2016, Mark 7:8). Because we have received the scouting report, the question becomes, what are we going to do to prepare to counter their intentions?

To View Opposition as Developmental Opportunities – 1 Timothy 4:12; 2 Timothy 4:17

When the testing of trials occurs, perspective and personality play an important role in how one navigates one's path. The optimist says the glass is half full, while the pessimist views the same glass as being half empty. A similar dynamic is involved when assessing the impact of challenges in the Christian's life. The challenges can stretch them or cause them to shrink back. Paul informed Timothy that everyone who desires to live a godly life will be persecuted (2 Timothy 3:12). When writing about 2 Timothy 3:12, Moşoiu (2019) focused on what it meant to suffer for living a godly life and concluded that the target of the persecutors was ultimately Jesus and the attacks would continue indefinitely. Since the writer of Hebrews was confident that the recipients of the book would not shrink back (Hebrews 10:39), we are going to exercise the same confidence and discuss a couple of perspectives of developmental opportunities opposition brings – opposition when watching the leader (leader as the learner's role model) and the leader's perspective while undergoing opposition (ideal introspection).

Learning from the Role Model

Timothy was Paul's traveling companion and ministry partner. Timothy witnessed Paul suffering persecution at Antioch, Iconium, and Lystra as they traveled. Paul realized and wrote that suffering of various types would happen to everyone who lived a godly lifestyle, but he was not attempting to scare Timothy or us. Moşoiu (2019) called the statement to Timothy and all who would believe an invitation to join in suffering. Jesus, the Master, suffered, and He declared that suffering with Him was vital to obtaining life (Matthew 16:25). Paul reiterated that thought when he reasoned that enduring the opposition of suffering would lead to reigning with Christ. Paul understood how important it was for him to endure all that he went through because he knew others were looking at him. His testimony was, "I endure everything for the sake of the elect" (*ESV*, 2001/2016, 2 Timothy 2:10). Paul knew Timothy was watching him, but he also knew the Ephesians would be watching Timothy. In all that Timothy endeavored to do, Paul encouraged him to be mindful that those watching him needed to see an example of godly living in every aspect of his lifestyle (1 Timothy 4:12). Christian role models turn the light on not only for the world to see their good deeds but so that their Brothers and Sisters might be encouraged and informed.

Ideal Introspection

Paul knew that Timothy was observing him and that the Ephesians would look at Timothy's response to what was happening around him. Timothy would have to be intentional in his self-examination. As we mentioned earlier, God's Word would be the standard against which Timothy must examine himself. Observing Paul's responses and remembering how Jesus responded would be essential in conducting his assessment. Let us revisit Timothy's learning experience in the context of him conducting an internal evaluation. Timothy had been with Paul when Paul revealed to those traveling with him that the Holy Spirit made it clear to him that every city he visited would either put him in prison or assault him physically and mentally (Acts 20:23). Yet Timothy witnessed that Paul continued ministering from city to city. Because Timothy was a student of the Word, he understood from James's writing that trying a person's faith produces commitment that would enable the tested person to mature in their relationship with God (James 1:3-4). Finally, Timothy had Jesus's example as He moved intentionally and purposefully to Jerusalem, not allowing anything or anyone to deter Him from accomplishing what His Father had given Him to do. God convinced Paul that He had begun a good work in him and would continue that work, by way of succession, until the day of Jesus's return (Philippians 1:6). Paul's insistence on perseverance highlighted the need for introspection. While Timothy noted the severity of the tribulations, he was also aware of the strength God provided to endure the suffering. Paul, James, and Jesus were role models for Timothy and helped him understand how God's grace was sufficient and strengthening in his times of enduring opposition.

MODULE THREE – LESSON TWO

CHALLENGES – WHO AND WHAT

Overview

- What makes people a challenge?
- What makes situations challenging?
- How does God use challenges to develop His leaders?

Lesson Objectives

- To contend without becoming contentious.
- To recognize and rectify relationships over religion.
- To uncover the benefits of grace and mercy.

Scripture Readings

- 1 Timothy 1:3-11, 2:9-15, 4:1-5, 12, 6:1-10
- 2 Timothy 3:1-9

KEY WORDS

Speculation
Dissension
Depraved

OVERVIEW

Water comes in three forms – liquid, solid, and gas. Their forms are different, but their substance is the same. The opposition Christians face is similar. Paul said that the Christian's struggle is spiritual and not against flesh and blood; humanly, you cannot see and interact with the source of the warfare, but the manifestations, flesh and blood, and situations involving flesh and blood are always active. Your job would not be so difficult if you could eliminate the people and the issues they initiate. There will always be people, and as God's Word has informed us, if you are in the world, you will face a variety of tribulations (John 16:33). The opposition will come from our enemies, without and within, and the situations in which you find yourself. Paul immediately described the Ephesian situation to Timothy as one that would have him on the defensive against teachers spreading lies, misstatements, and other heretical statements causing confusion, generating speculation, and introducing controversial doctrines (Bond, 2006). Some of the people were from the outside, like Alexander (2 Timothy 4:14); some swerved from within, like Philetus (2 Timothy 2:17); and others, like Hymenaeus and Alexander, were undergoing discipline (Thornton, 2015). Regardless of their status, they all presented an oppositional stance to the growth and development of the Ephesian believers or an obstacle to the presentation of the gospel. Through it all, James assured his readers that God uses these challenges to make His followers "perfect and complete, lacking nothing" (*ESV*, 2001/2016, James 1:4). God's work in His people is an ongoing work completed only when Jesus comes again. So, keep fighting the good fight of faith.

OBJECTIVES: LESSON TWO

To Contend Without Becoming Contentious – 2 Timothy 2:24

The challenges of assimilation related to association are real in that people tend to become like the folks they hang around. Solomon encouraged his son to spend time with wise people so that he could become wise and cautioned him about spending time with fools (Proverbs 13:20). The real challenge, though, was having the discernment to know when and how to respond to those caught in the quicksand of folly (Proverbs 26:4-5). We have seen that those not on Timothy's team were all around him, presenting challenges and putting him into situations where his natural tendency would be to refrain from engaging or over-engaging. As God's representative, though, he could not allow opponents of the truths of God's Word to go unchallenged. Still, Paul admonished him that as God's representative, he should not be argumentative. As Van Neste (2022) pointed out, your primary purpose for using words is not to win arguments but to point people to the way of repentance. Contending without becoming contentious requires a commitment to the lifelong pursuit of refinement.

Timothy was a relatively young man in that those he led were more chronologically seasoned. MacDonald (1990) suggested that Timothy may have tended to be impatient with those older than him and aggressive with those younger than him. Instead of following the norms, Paul insisted that he use words respectfully when addressing those more senior than him, his peers, and those younger as if they were siblings. Van Neste (2022) noted that many seminarians unwittingly have a pride issue that causes them to be quarrelsome and aggressive with people of lesser learning or knowledge. In the referenced verse, Paul admonished Timothy to be patient with those who were slow to understand and those who were resistant to the truth

(MacDonald, 1990). The temptation may be to misuse words and cause the discussions to be more about words than pointing people to Jesus.

What is the path that avoids becoming quarrelsome and confrontational? Four times in these letters to Timothy, Paul challenges him to avoid or have nothing to do with irreverent, silly, foolish, ignorant conversations (1 Timothy 4:7; 6:20; 2:16; 2:23). Too many times, leaders feel compelled to get involved or to respond to every comment and become entangled in messy situations that are not God-honoring or uplifting to our Brothers and Sisters. Van Neste (2022) modernized Paul's caution to Timothy when he mentioned that most of these communications occur electronically on various social media platforms. Many people use social media platforms to obtain more information without acknowledging the truth (2 Timothy 3:7). Your responsibility is to teach, not argue, with the understanding that it is God, through His Holy Spirit, that guides the opposition to a place of repentance and acknowledgment of the truth (2 Timothy 2:24). Contending without becoming contentious is a Holy Spirit taught skill that gets refined as we live life with those whom God has created in His image and likeness but have chosen to be on the other team.

To Recognize and Rectify Relationships over Religion – 1 Timothy 1:5

When Paul was visiting Athens, he spent some time with the great Athenian thinkers and noted how religious they were. Without disparaging their religion, Paul reasoned with them to bring them to the point of understanding the greater importance of relationships over religion (Acts 17:22-31). In the same way, Paul wanted Timothy to comprehend that the goal of the mission he had given him in the previous verses was to produce love (MacDonald, 1990). Paul gave Timothy an extensive mission encompassing many points of emphasis, but Heringer (2021) stated that

Paul wanted him to know up front that it was all about love. Timothy would have to feed some points to the Ephesians that would be difficult to swallow, but feed them he must – but as acts of love, not condemnation with an attitude of anger. As the writer of Hebrews made clear, God demonstrates His love for His people by disciplining them, and those not disciplined by God are not His children (Hebrews 12:5-8). When instructing the Ephesians, God would challenge Timothy to speak to the rock and not strike it in anger.

There was no shortage of religious teachings in Ephesus. There were teachers of mythology and genealogy (1 Timothy 1:4), teachers who thought they understood the Mosaic law (1 Timothy 1:7), teachers propagating demonic, deceitful practices (1 Timothy 4:1), teachers pandering to please the people (2 Timothy 4:3), and those who were engaging in irreverent, foolish babblings (1 Timothy 6:20). In 2006, the Yearbook of *American and Canadian Churches* listed nearly 220 denominations with many more churches aligning themselves with various non-denominational organizations. Wherever God's people meet, though, the foundational motive must be love because if the motivation is anything other than love, 1 Corinthians 13:1-3 calculated the value of those meetings – nothing. Today, many are teaching a variety of doctrines with many underlying motives that may or may not stem from a genuine love of God or those created in His image and likeness.

James provided an accurate picture of religion, which has intricate relationships interwoven. Ziglar (2003) noted that James 1:27 provided two means of maintaining one's relationship with God – 1) taking care of those orphans and widows who have limited means to provide for themselves and 2) distancing themselves from the ways of the world. In 1 John 2:15, John made it clear that loving the world and loving God are mutually exclusive. John's writing reinforced Jesus's proclamation from the mountain that man can only serve God or money – not both. Paul's desire for Timothy and those who would later read his letter was that the readers would recognize the overarching, eternal supremacy of godliness and prioritize godliness over the temporary benefits of earthly pursuits (1 Timothy 4:7-8). Being religious in a manner acceptable to God is not a naturally occurring combination of religion and relationship but requires "exercise and effort" (MacDonald, 1990, p. 908). Paul challenged Timothy to convey to the Ephesians that they were to do good, be generous, and be ready to share (1 Timothy 6:18). This lesson is relevant today. Instead of just talking about it, believers must be about it – doing what is needed to practice religion in a way that is pleasing to God.

To Uncover the Benefits of Grace and Mercy – 2 Timothy 4:16

As the chief of sinners, Paul was also a thankful recipient of God's grace. There was nothing Paul had done to merit the grace he received from God. Jesus said that what the disciples received freely, they should give freely (Matthew 10:8). Jesus had come to the world to save sinners, and when He saved Paul, he realized that he "received mercy" and that the "grace of our Lord overflowed for [him]" (*ESV*, 2001/2016, 1 Timothy 1:13-14). Your story may not be Paul's, but none of our stories merits God's saving grace and mercy since while we were sinners, Christ paid the price for sin on the cross of Calvary.

As we represent Christ to the world, our opposition is out to stop us from carrying out our God-assigned mission to preach the gospel. Paul wanted his readers to be aware of the massive task we must complete, but he did not want us to think we had to finish it using our resources. Timothy witnessed firsthand Paul's response to suffering, but Paul documented various opponents throughout his letters to Timothy. When he gets to the conclusion of his letters, Paul mentions that Alexander has been the source of trouble for him. MacDonald (1990) speculated that Alexander may have testified about Paul falsely and brought false charges against him. Note Paul's response in 2 Timothy 4:16. His forgiving response was one from someone who has received gracious, merciful forgiveness. His response was attentive and obedient to Jesus's words, "Love your enemies and pray for those who persecute you" (ESV, 2001/2016, Matthew 5:44). Thank God! His grace and mercy provide a remedy for those who oppose us; however, He requires recipients to submit to His authority.

MODULE THREE – LESSON THREE

OVERCOMING THE COMPLEXITIES OF LEADERSHIP

Overview

- To be forewarned is to be forearmed.
- Learning from our examples, i.e., Jesus and Paul.

Lesson Objectives

- To urge and request prayer.
- To diligently study and practice.
- To understand who you are as a person serving a leadership position with a specific purpose.

Scripture Readings

- 1 Timothy 3:1-13, 4:12-13, 6:1-10

Key Words

Doctrine	Bondservants
Content	

OVERVIEW

Living the Christian life is challenging, and leading God's people is even more difficult. You have explored why there are challenges and the composition of the opposition. During this lesson, you will focus on methodologies to overcome the complexities of leadership as prescribed by Paul in his letters to his protégé Timothy. As mentioned earlier, we do not want you to be surprised by the conflicts you encounter as you begin leading God's people. Remember, our Master, Jesus, had to overcome the same challenges you will face, and He did so. Some may say that because He was God wrapped in human flesh, they would not expect any less than Him defeating the forces of evil with whom He clashed. In this lesson, we will also examine Paul in all his humanity and how he endured persecution and suffering, leaving a roadmap you can study and practice as you strive to become who God has called you to be.

You are coming close to embarking on a special time of service that requires preparation. Jesus came and lived on earth for thirty-three years while all the time anticipating the time when He would have to suffer and die for the sins He did not commit and pay the price humans could not pay. He understood the gravity of what was about to happen, and as physically painful as it would be, He said, "For this purpose I have come to this hour" (*ESV*, 2001/2016, John 12:27). He knew He would experience physical pain and the pain of denial from His Father. However, when the time came, Luke recorded that Jesus was unflinchingly determined to face the challenge ahead of Him in Jerusalem (Luke 9:51). Earlier, a crowd was going to throw Jesus down a cliff, but as Jensen (2021) described

Luke 4:30, Jesus in His gentle presence and the power of the Holy Spirit somehow went on His way to complete His earthly mission. He knew He would face opposition, was prepared, and did not allow anything to prevent Him from reaching His appointed time and accomplishing his divine objective.

Then, consider Paul as you prepare to face the world's tribulations. Upon his conversion on the road to Damascus, God let Ananias know that Saul, the persecutor, would go from persecuting to being Paul, the object of maltreatment. Ananias had the unenviable task of being around when God showed Saul that he would be the one to take the gospel to the Gentiles and suffer because of that decision (Acts 9:15-16). Along the way, Paul connected with Timothy, and Timothy became an eyewitness to Paul's persecutions and sufferings in Antioch, Iconium, and Lystra (2 Timothy 3:11). With an eye toward the close of his ministry, Idowu (2017) posited Paul's warning to a next-generation leader, Timothy, that tough times were ahead and that things would go from bad to worse as "challenges to the faith develop[ed] from within" (p. 94). As you continue with this FMIFC process, you must remember to have and continually develop the spirit to urgently seek God and understand who He has called you to be and to become.

OBJECTIVES: LESSON THREE

To Urge and Request Prayer

The lyrics of a song I heard the other day mentioned that if some folks did not experience difficulties, they would never pray. How many of you have listened to someone recall that things got so bad that all they could do was pray? Well, the truth is, prayer must be option number one. As we look at these methodologies to overcome the complexities of leadership, the FMIFC process prioritizes prayer.

Look at Jesus

Jesus, God's Son, prioritized prayer in His life so much that it is one of the practices He intentionally taught and modeled for them. Matthew recorded Him teaching His followers how to pray (Matthew 6:9). Mark included an instance of Jesus prioritizing prayer in preparation for preaching (Mark 1:35-38). In Luke, His disciples requested that He teach them how to pray (Luke 11:1). John 17 preserved for posterity what has become known as Jesus's high priestly prayer when Jesus prays for His current followers and for those who would believe in Him because His current followers would faithfully spread the word. After Jesus died, resurrected, ascended, and sat at the right hand of His Father, the writer of Hebrews informed us that "He lives to make intercession" for us (*ESV*, 2001/2016, Hebrews 7:25). Jesus is interceding for us because He knows the strong opposition His people face. When they faced that opposition, He gave directions about what to do. As counter-cultural as it seemed and seems, Searle (2009) argued that praying for those persecuting you was evidence of loving one's enemies, and though it was difficult, it is not impossible. While hanging on the cross, Jesus prayed to His Father to forgive those who were crucifying Him.

Look at Paul

When Paul provided instructions for Timothy, he specified the priority of actions. MacDonald (1990) called attention to the likelihood of Paul instructing in 1 Timothy 2 for public prayers and noted that what was suitable for public prayer was not out of line for his private prayer life. Praying must be at the top of Timothy's list and include various prayers for all people – including secular leaders (Evans & Holman, 2019). It seems reasonable to believe Paul was also making a personal request for prayer because he continued, later in the passage, stating that his "desire" was for men everywhere to pray (*ESV*, 2001/2016, 1 Timothy 2:8). Evans and

Holman (2019) emphasized the necessity of prayer when they described it as people on earth asking heaven to intervene in history. While there will be tribulation, God's people must believe, like the Hebrew boys of Daniel 3:17, that God can deliver His people when they call. Paul, writing to the believers in Ephesus, encouraged them by letting them know that God could do much more than they could think, dream, or even imagine (Ephesians 3:20). Calling God for His involvement must be option number one.

To Diligently Study and Practice

God's Word described Solomon's wisdom and discernment as humanly unapproachable (1 Kings 3:12). It is then interesting that Solomon taught his people the importance of studying (Ecclesiastes 12:9) and then described studying as "a weariness of the flesh" (*ESV*, 2001/2016, Ecclesiastes 12:12). When using a sporting analogy, though, opposing teams study each other's plays, repeatedly going over them, and noting trends that potentially will give them a situational edge. After studying, they practice what they must do to succeed in those situations.

Look at Jesus

Jesus was very observant of the opposition – physically and spiritually. The religious leaders of His day were constantly attempting to put Him in a situation to accuse Him of violating their laws and customs. In Matthew 23, He called out the scribes and Pharisees as hypocrites (vv. 13, 15, 23, 25, 27, 29) and blind guides (vv. 16, 17, 19, 24, 26). He had studied their plays and summarized their actions for His disciples, "They preach, but do not practice" (ESV, 2001/2016, Matthew 23:3). In John's account of His encounters with the religious leaders, Jesus pointed out their family heritage and customs when He told them they were acting like their father the devil and speaking in the devil's native language, lies (John 8: 44). Conversely, Jesus went about doing His Father's business and proving His love of His Father by completing all the Father commanded Him to do (John 14:31). Jesus lived a life of selfless service (MacDonald, 1990). Although He was God, He emptied Himself, became a man, and then suffered an unwarranted death on the cross (Philippians 2:8). Jesus knew what He needed to do, did it, and in doing so, left an example for us to follow (1 Peter 2:21).

Look at Paul

What an incredible history Paul had. His testimony of strict Jewish religiosity was that he had been "circumcised on the eighth day, of the people of Israel, of the tribe of Benjamin, a Hebrew of Hebrews; as to the law, a Pharisee; as to zeal, a persecutor of the church; as to righteousness under the law, blameless" (*ESV*, 2001/2016, Philippians 3:5-6). On another occasion, Paul informed his audience that he studied under the much-respected Jewish Elder, Gamaliel (Acts 22:3). There was no question of Paul's pedigree or practice, so no one should be surprised that after his conversion to The Way his mode of learning did not change nor was his zeal for that which he believed.

Paul encouraged Timothy to study diligently to be scholarly and a good teacher. There were many teachers in Ephesus; however, what they were teaching did not meet the qualifications for good. Paul, as a master trainer, invested in his spiritual son, Timothy (Engstrom, 1978). In subsequent writings to Timothy, Paul encouraged Timothy to continue the lessons learned and believed because he knew from whom he had learned the teachings (2 Timothy 3:14) and had firsthand experience watching Paul's manner of life and how it matched his preaching, teaching, and writings. MacDonald (1990) suggested a study methodology that included exhortation (application) and doctrinal teaching to the church. Timothy would have had to complete extensive reading and private study to excel in these areas. Paul clarified to Timothy that studying and speaking were intricate parts of communicating truth; however, the Ephesians needed to see the results of the studying, teaching, and preaching lived out.

An old saying states that practice makes perfect; some have modified that statement to say that perfect practice makes perfect. Either way, Paul wanted Timothy to publicly put into practice the habits he was preparing in private. Dionson (2015) compared Paul's encouragement to practice to a coach prodding a protégé to commit to doing everything needed to become fully immersed and committed to excellence. As the leader, Timothy would be on display, modeling for the church the behaviors they should emulate (1 Timothy 3:15; 4:12). The only way to get better at an activity is the repetitive practice of that activity in varying environments comparable to the locus of praxis. Considering Timothy's role in the Ephesian church, Lawson (2002) posited that practicing reading, exhortation, and teaching would enable Timothy and his hearers to accurately apply the Word based on the deliberate delivery of doctrine.

To Understand You Are a Person Serving in a Leadership Position with a Specific Purpose

Sometimes, God designates a person for leadership when that person is not aware of their God-given abilities. A prime example is Moses, the man God chose to lead His people out of the bondage of slavery in Egypt before he was born (Psalm 139:16). Here is a quick overview of God's sovereign intervention in his life – God spared him from death at birth, his mother recognized something special in the child she bore (Exodus 2:2), and the Pharaoh's daughter paid his mother to nurse him (Exodus 2:9). Later, God miraculously appeared to him in a burning bush that was not consumed by the fire (Exodus 3:2). When God told Moses that he was the person designated to go to Pharaoh, Moses immediately developed either an inferiority complex or was extremely humble because he doubted why God would select him. Moses made excuse after excuse – The Israelites will not believe me or listen to me (Exodus 4:1); I am not a skilled speaker, and I have a slow tongue (Exodus 4:10). Even after God reminded him that He was the maker and designer of the mouth and language, Moses begged God, "Please send someone else" (*ESV*, 2001/2016, Exodus 4:13). How many times do we hesitate to do God's bidding? Blackaby et al. (2023) advised immediate obedience to anything God tells you to do. Ammer (2013) paraphrased an old proverb by noting that hesitation is characteristic of unbelief and uncertainty. Moses should have replaced unbelief and uncertainty with confidence and courage when God introduced Himself as the God of his fathers, Abraham, Isaac, and Jacob. This section will focus on how Jesus and Paul's understanding of who they were drove their actions, awareness, and attitude as they faced adversity.

Look at Jesus

Many people are more aware of John 3:16 than the following verse. Verse seventeen expresses the reason Jesus left the splendor and glory of heaven to come to earth – "that the world might be saved through Him" (*ESV*, 2001/2016, John 3:17). He went to the people who had the same ethno-religious background; however, they did not recognize who He was or the reason for his visitation which caused them to mistreat Him and ultimately kill Him (Luke 19:44). There are a couple of examples which demonstrate Jesus's knowledge of who He was and His purpose. Luke recorded His earthly parents taking Him to the temple early in His life when He was twelve. When His parents unwittingly left Jesus there, they were surprised when they returned to the temple and found Him conversing with the teachers. At this point, Jesus expressed his awareness of who He was. There is a variance of opinion about the translation of what Jesus replied. Sylva (1987) contended that Jesus said either 1) He had to be in His Father's house, 2) about His Father's affairs, or 3) with those belonging to My Father (pp. 133-134). Another scholar, Temple (1939), argued for the translation to be "house" or "business" and concluded that Jesus was informing His parents that He had to be involved in promoting the interests of His Father (pp. 349-350). Whether it was His Father's house, business, interests, or Word, as a young man, Jesus recognized that His Father had given Him a task, and He was committed to completing the assignment out of love.

Another instance of Jesus's recognition of who He was and what He came to do was near the end of His physical life, as Pilate privately interviewed Jesus. As Pilate was querying Jesus, Jesus took the opportunity to specify who He was and His purpose – a king and a communicator of truth (John 18:36-37). As Jesus communicated truth to Pilate, Brown (2015) connected Jesus's responses to Pilate to His Father, who was the source of all the power Pilate thought he had assumed because of his accomplishments. Pilate also made a connection between Jesus's words and His Father, as evidenced by his realization that Jesus's identity was more of an issue than the charges the Jews brought against Him (Brown, 2015). The people's false accusations would ultimately lead to His crucifixion. However, it would not be before Pilate (Luke 19:19-22), one of the thieves crucified with Him (Luke 23:40), and a centurion (Matthew 27:54, Mark 15:39) would recognize who He was. In His high priestly prayer, Jesus provided His eulogy, "I glorified You on earth, having accomplished the work You gave me to do" (*ESV*, 2001/2016, John 17: 4). In recognition of Jesus's humility, suffering, and completed work, Paul noted in Philippians 2:8 that Jesus obeyed His Father to death on a cross without regard to the shame associated with dying on a cross. As the songwriters Hall and Bleeker succinctly put it, "My example is He."

Look at Paul

Jesus was the inspirational example who moved Paul to write the theme for this FMIFC process. Paul challenged himself and those who would read his writings to "Be imitators of me, as I am of Christ" (*ESV*, 2001/2016, 1 Corinthians 11:1). Almost immediately after his conversion, Paul came under attack. God had informed Ananias of the suffering Paul would endure to carry out his assignment to the Gentiles and the people of Israel. After Paul saw the light and began bearing witness to that light, the Jews with whom he previously associated became agitated by his change of heart and planned to kill him (Acts 9:23). God, though, had other plans. God had revealed Paul's trying future to Ananias. Still, He also told Paul that in every city he would visit, he would be in prison, or the people would physically mistreat him (Acts 20:23). The irony of the revelation was that Paul received it in Ephesus and Ephesus would be where he would assign Timothy to minister.

Would it not be great to know whether Ananias shared with Paul what God shared with him about what the future held for Paul? Moessner (1986) posited suffering as a requirement to be a prophet of God as he connected the sufferings of Peter, Stephen, and Paul to the sufferings of Jesus Christ. Paul then expanded on this concept when he noted that everyone who wanted to live a godly life pleasing to Jesus would suffer persecution (2 Timothy 3:12). In 2 Timothy 3, Paul is preparing Timothy to live the life Timothy witnessed Paul living. In the previous verse, 2 Timothy 3:11, Paul specified the sufferings that Timothy saw in Antioch, Iconium, and Lystra. He was telling Timothy what he had to look forward to. Earlier in this letter, Paul had explained to Timothy his resolve in suffering because God had convinced Paul of His call on his and Timothy's life to this work before either was born, conceived, or thought of (2 Timothy 1:9). Not only was Paul convinced, but he was also committed to its completion. Like Jesus, Paul provided some words for his eulogy, "I have fought the good fight, I have finished the race, I have kept the faith" (*ESV*, 2001/2016, 2 Timothy 4:7). After being convicted, Paul lived a life fully convinced of his calling and Caller and fully committed to accomplishing his assigned mission.

Look at You

Well, you have received the warning – The road ahead is paved with tribulation and trouble because your Master faced it, and you are not greater than your Master. Luke recorded that Paul, our senior guide through the FMIFC process, said this in Lystra, one of the towns Timothy witnessed him getting stoned and left for dead, "Through many tribulations we must enter the kingdom of God" (*ESV*, 2001/2016, Acts 14:22). You know the playbook of your adversary the devil. He has designed every play to steal your joy, kill your enthusiasm, and destroy whatever you have left. What a daunting scenario this presents. Let the words of Jim Elliott encourage you as you fight the good fight of faith, "He is no fool who gives what he cannot keep, to gain what he cannot lose." God, the God of Abraham, Isaac, Jacob, and all the people you consider people of God, is on your side, bidding you to do the work prepared for you that He has designed you to do.

MODULE 4

THE CHARGES TO LEADERSHIP

MODULE INTRODUCTION

Welcome to the fourth and final module of the FMIFC curriculum process. In this module, we will be covering the Challenges of Leadership. Again, we will focus on Paul's writings to Timothy, but this time, focusing on the personal challenges for Timothy to live up to and the preaching challenges Timothy would have to institute to keep the Ephesian church accountable to each other and God. As always, there are expectations placed upon leaders to model for their followers, and additionally, there are enforcement responsibilities that accompany the privileges of leadership. We will begin by defining the three types of charges mentioned in the writings and move on to the charges Paul gave to Timothy to govern his personal life before concluding with the preaching and teaching charges Paul gave to Timothy to manage his leadership accountability. This module contains only two lessons. Below is an overview of the content we will cover during this segment.

Module Four Overview

	Lesson One: A Charge to Keep	**Lesson Two:** A Charge to Give
Overview:	* Paul expected Timothy to set an example for the believers in preaching and practice. * Timothy had a level of proficiency that he had to perfect through practice.	* Leaders require accountability of those they lead. * Discipline and punishment are the other side of love.
Objectives:	* To live up to your leadership calling. * To develop and display godly character. * To guide the navigation of challenges.	* To demonstrate love in the exercise of leadership. * To submit to the accountability of leadership. * To eliminate evil practices and establish godly patterns.
Scripture Readings:	1 Timothy 1:5, 17-19, 5:18-22, 2 Timothy 4:1-2	1 Timothy 1:2-4, 5, 6:16-18, 2 Timothy 2:13-14
Vocabulary/Key Words:	Charge, shipwreck, charge, reprove	Speculations, faith, haughty, quarrel

MODULE FOUR – LESSON ONE

A CHARGE TO KEEP

Overview

- Paul expected Timothy to set an example for the believers in preaching and practice.
- Timothy had a level of proficiency that he had to perfect through practice.

Lesson Objectives

- To live up to your leadership calling.
- To develop and display godly character.
- To guide the navigation of challenges.

Scripture Readings

- 1 Timothy 1:5, 17-19, 5:18-22, 2 Timothy 4:1-2

KEY WORDS

Charge	Shipwreck
Charge	Reprove

OVERVIEW

One of the first things that happens to an Officer in the military upon taking a new assignment is sitting down with the Commander and discussing the job description, requirements, and expectations. Commanders then share the same type of documentation their higher authority expects. At the end of the discussion, incoming Officers know their responsibilities and how their supervisor intends for them to be effective, and they have an overview of the guidance their supervisor's supervisor has given them. Timothy already knew that Paul had set the tone for those who looked to him for leadership with his message to the Corinthian church, "Follow my example, as I follow the example of Christ" (*NIV*, 1978/1984, 1 Corinthians 11:1). Additionally, as one of Paul's travel companions, Timothy had traveled extensively with Paul viewing firsthand his personal devotional life, interactions with individuals, interactions with churches, sufferings at the hands of the opposition, betrayal by some within the body of Christ, and participated in authoring of some of Paul's letters to the churches. Timothy was familiar with Jesus's works and followed Paul's works, and now it was time for him to fulfill the works God prepared in advance for him to do.

To get Timothy started on his leadership journey, Paul gave Timothy charges. Translators rendered several words as a form of charge; however, we will use the English translations and categorize them as either a legal term, the transmission of a command, or the command transmitted. In 1 Timothy 5:19 and 2 Timothy 4:16, the term implies some judgment – in the first instance, the word suggests an accusation against an elder. In contrast, in the second verse, the word is used so that those making the judgment, a reckoning, do not do so against a violator. The variations of charge covered in the following objectives relate to transmitting a message from Paul to Timothy (personal) or from Timothy to the Ephesians (pastoral). Because it is a charge, there is a sense of urgency and priority in delivering the message. These charges are not suggestions that the receivers may carry out as an option. Instead, they are commands that communicate supervisor to those supervised. If those under supervision desire a favorable assessment, they will need to fulfill the demands of the charge.

OBJECTIVES: LESSON ONE

To Live Up to Your Leadership Calling – 1 Timothy 1:18

In any undertaking, knowing and understanding the why of the mission is a crucial motivational factor one may rely on – especially when fear and doubt assail. When Paul addressed the Corinthian church about exercising their gifts, he made it clear in 1 Corinthians 13 how and why they should use them. After reasoning, Paul concluded that faith, hope, and love are three factors that withstood the rigors of time and circumstances. Although these three remained, Paul declared, "The greatest of these is love" (*ESV*, 2001/2016, 1 Corinthians 13:13). Consistent with the three remaining virtues, Paul communicated charges for Timothy to carry out in his role with the Ephesian church. The overarching aim is love (1 Timothy 1:5), but Morgan (1987) argued that faith and hope are enduring qualities for consideration. Some would say that seeing does away with faith and satisfaction replaces hope, but Paul, under the inspiration of the Holy Spirit, stated they remain (Morgan, 1987). When Paul began his letters to Timothy, his introduction included hope, love, and faith. The authority granted to Paul for authoritatively documenting this epistle came from

God and His Son, Jesus, who is our hope (1 Timothy 1:1). Love is the 'why' of Paul's charges to Timothy. Still, the catalyst for Paul's love was his genuine faith in God's Son (1 Timothy 1:5), which MacDonald (1990) posited included an honest love of God and other believers. Paul's deep love and affection for his spiritual son drove him to provide personal charges for Timothy.

The focus of the FMIFC process is for the leader to set an example for the learner(s) to follow. Of the five leadership practices Kouzes and Posner (2017) detailed, modeling the way was the primary responsibility of the one who would lead. Setting the example requires the leader to live by values expressed and fleshed out so that followers can associate the virtue with actions applied to situations (Kouzes & Posner, 2017). Paul charged Timothy to live up to his leadership calling by reminding him of an event from his past in the referenced verse. MacDonald (1990) speculated that somewhere in Timothy's past, a prophet publicly communicated to Timothy God's grand plans for his spiritual future, so he should recall the prophecy in times of discouragement and depression. Willimon (2016) noted that the act's symbology represented the Holy Spirit's impartation for Timothy to have the authority of the person who recognized his gift. If Timothy would remember the words spoken over him, he would be mindful of the armor and armament the Holy Spirit provided to overcome the challenges he would encounter (Beale, 2023). Recalling the words would guide Timothy's actions and attitudes, enabling him to maintain his "faith and a good conscience" as he battled the temptations to give up the faith because of the difficulties he encountered (*ESV*, 2001/2016, 1 Timothy 1:19). People in Ephesus would be watching this young man so Paul's commands to Timothy included modeling for the church of how they should speak, act, love, demonstrate their faithfulness, and maintain their sexual purity. MacDonald (1990) clarified the importance of Timothy modeling these characteristics to minimize the possibilities of unjust criticism. As the leader, Timothy's teaching would not be enough; he would have to model the truths he taught that aligned with the authority he received when the prophet spoke over him and the elders laid their hands on him.

Just as in Timothy's time, there will be leaders whose walk does not match their talk. In the next lesson, there will be messages Paul charged Timothy to preach to the Ephesians, but those messages would be in vain, falling on deaf ears if Timothy behaved like the Pharisees Jesus described in Matthew 23. As you near completion of this process, there is a need for anamnesis – a recollection of the lessons provided in the FMIFC process about authenticity in your leadership role. You cannot fail to use the gifts that the laying on of hands will signify and confirm that you have within you. Your age cannot be a deterrent for you to not authentically demonstrate the stewardship of your gift(s) by using them faithfully (1 Corinthians 4:2). The things Paul wrote to Timothy were for your learning and modeling, so you must be careful to do as instructed resulting in a blessing for you and to those listening to you. Your effectiveness as a leader depends on living up to your calling by developing and strengthening your relationship with God so that no one can call your character into question.

To Develop and Display Godly Character – 1 Timothy 5:21 and 6:13

In Module Two, we delved into the essential nature of having a godly character and some definitions and descriptions of what a godly character looks like. In this module lesson, the focus is on Paul charging Timothy to have character beyond reproach. Once again, it is vital to note Paul is not giving Timothy options for consideration but commands for implementation. Paul described to Timothy what this would look like as he laid out the prerequisites for being an elder and, at the apex of the characteristics, insisted the elder must have a sterling reputation with outsiders (1 Timothy 3:7). Evans and Holman (2019) insisted elders must be highly regarded and have the respect of unbelievers because they live a life marked with character and integrity. In 1 Timothy 5, Paul addressed Timothy's behavior within the church relating to older and younger men, older and younger women, and elders by commanding him to be impartial – especially as it pertained to entertaining accusations against elders (Strauch, 2009). Partiality in judgment was a common discriminatory practice that the law prohibited (Leviticus 19:15), and James disdained (James 2).

Additionally, Paul reminded Timothy that he was under the same authority as Paul – God was the witness. There are several possibilities for the charge Paul issued to Timothy to keep the commandment in 1 Timothy 6:13. It is likely a comprehensive charge again reminding Timothy that he was responsible before God (1 Timothy 6:11) and that his life's actions must reflect righteousness, godliness, faith, love, steadfastness, and gentleness to avoid the reproach of those witnessing his lifestyle (Evans & Holman, 2019). Several people have received credit for noting that character is who you are when no one is watching. Still, Coach John Wooden went deeper by drilling into his players the higher importance of character over reputation. Character is who you are, while your reputation is only what people think you are. Scripture says that your unreproachable reputation and leaders of God's people must always display character.

As mentioned earlier, Timothy was new to the Ephesian church as a leader, and as his relationship with the church changed, so did the church's expectations of Timothy. You may have previously served in another capacity in the church where you are or will assume leadership. Immediately after Paul experienced conversion, his reputation preceded him, creating doubt in the minds of the believers in Damascus. It was difficult for them to make the mental transition to accept as a partner in the faith the person who previously persecuted them because of their faith. Similarly, Hull (1959) determined that Timothy had experienced an unfruitful tenure with the Corinthian church, which caused Paul to direct Timothy to stay at his post in Ephesus, to remind Timothy of the authority under which he was serving, and to command him to be steadfast in the Ephesian endeavor. With the challenges Timothy experienced, it is important to note Paul's companionship of Timothy as his mentor, his supporter, and an endorser of His ability to execute his calling effectively (Hull, 1959). Each leader has a past that may have been terrific or terrible. Regardless, when God has called you to leadership, there are times when you must grow into your responsibility. Peter denied Christ three times, but Jesus told him that when he turned back, his responsibility would be to strengthen his brothers (Luke 22:32). Peter understood the need to grow in one's faith and knowledge of their Savior. Later, he encouraged that growth in other believers (2 Peter 3:18). Paul's encouragement of Timothy not to be hindered by fear (2 Timothy 1:7) but to be strengthened by studying (2 Timothy 2:15) and practicing his faith (1 Timothy 4:15). You will maximize your potential for effective service as you refuse to continue building monuments to your past and choose to be a living testimony of God's grace and mercy.

TO GUIDE THE NAVIGATION OF CHALLENGES – 2 TIMOTHY 4:1-2

Paul's commands to Timothy to live up to his calling by living a life characterized by godliness would supplement the words from Timothy's mouth. Paul did not beat around the bush in his direction to Timothy. He gave him the prescription for the ills impacting the Ephesian church – "Preach the word" (*ESV*, 2001/2016, 2 Timothy 4:2). What higher calling could one have than to preach God's Word to those created in His image and likeness – saved and unsaved? Paul questioned how a person can come to know Christ without someone preaching (Romans 10:14), and then in the referenced passage, Paul noted when preaching should occur and what the content of the sermons should include. Zorn (1991) advised that if preachers would like to finish as well as Paul did in his testimony in verses 7-8, they would have to take the medication as prescribed in the text. The preacher must present the word when it is convenient and inconvenient. To fulfill the intent of the prescription, heavy doses of the Word will generate salvation for the lost, engender fruitful living for the saved, remedy the sinful practices of the carnal, and counter the false doctrines of the false teachers (Zorn, 1991). This narrow prescription was intentional because the road to destruction is broad.

Timothy could only provide the unadulterated true path as he followed the guidance of Scripture. Paul noted Timothy's spiritual upbringing centered on the sacred writings (1 Timothy 3:15), and he was familiar with Paul because of their partnership in the gospel (1 Timothy 3:14). In Timothy's case, familiarity did not breed contempt, but instead, it instilled confidence. Paul emphasized to Timothy that only Scripture came from the breath of God. As such, Scripture was the only positioning system that would enable safe passage through the deep, murky waters of false doctrines, abuse of the law, liars, godlessness, and babbling. Mayes (2019) focused on Scripture as the source of reproof – refuting that which is false doctrine. Expanding on reproof, Mayes (2019) cautioned, like Solomon, that there was a time for everything, and every sermon with any audience is not necessarily the right time to exercise reproof. One must not be silent, but one must be discerning because there are times when such reproof would leave the less mature, minimally informed believer more confused than edified (Mayes, 2019).

Some preachers spend more time on the newspaper's front page and various social media posts than they do in the Word. The prescription calls for the Word, and the global positioning system points singularly to the Word. Always use God's Word as the authoritative source for preaching when you must correct errors, disapprove of behaviors, or provide doctrinal instructions. Remember to preach the word with patience to the listener. As Peter cautioned, instruct with gentleness and respect (1 Peter 3:15). There is no better authoritative source than God's Word. Psalm 119 is replete with reasons to use Scripture, with Psalm 119:89 forming the basis – God's Word is firm, fixed, and forever in the heavens. Any other source will change as situations and the people around them change. Preach the Word, not the front page of the newspaper.

MODULE FOUR – LESSON TWO

A CHARGE TO GIVE

Overview

- Leaders require accountability of those they lead.
- Discipline and punishment are the other side of love.

Lesson Objectives

- To demonstrate love in the exercise of leadership.
- To submit to the accountability of leadership.
- To eliminate evil practices and establish godly patterns.

Scripture Readings

- 1 Timothy 1:2-4, 5, 6:16-18, 2 Timothy 2:13-14

Key Words

Speculations	Faith
Haughty	Quarrel

OVERVIEW

Leadership Accountability

Viewing the learner-leader models is like the leader-follower models with multiple definitions, descriptions, and theories. For simplicity's sake, this view of accountability will use McGregor's Theory X and Theory Y, which some say are overly simplified leadership theory models, but which McGregor saw as options from which a leader may choose. Theory X leaders assume a disinterested workforce with minimal initiative requiring close supervision. Conversely, Theory Y leaders believe they have a happy, imaginative workforce committed to developing solutions to satisfy organizational needs (Hackman & Johnson, 2013). Regardless of their approach or industry, leaders are responsible for ensuring the accomplishment of organizational goals. Northouse (2019) defined leadership as a process an individual (leader) uses to influence individuals (followers) to accomplish agreed-upon goals. The writer of Hebrews encouraged followers to obey and submit to their leaders because those in leadership bear the responsibility of having to give an account for work assigned to their organization (Hebrews 13:17). So, there must be standards in place guiding work accomplishment (learner) and gauging the quality of work achievement (leader).

No one was more aware of the challenges of leadership accountability than Paul. When writing to the Roman believers, he cautioned that everyone is subject to the authority granted to leadership, that God is the source of all authority, and that those who disobey authority will suffer the consequences (Romans 13:1-2). With that understanding, Paul gave Timothy some commands for his submission, and now we will look at some commands Paul gave to Timothy to pass on to the Ephesian church. Some Ephesians required Theory X leadership, so Timothy would have to lay down the law very strictly because they considered themselves a law to themselves, disobeying and misusing God's law (1 Timothy 1:8-10). There were also members of the Ephesian church busily engaged in work; however, they needed attitude adjustments to reorient their efforts. Paul clarified to Timothy that setting the Ephesian church in order was why he was to take up residence in Ephesus. Maybe God will place you in such a setting. Do not run away, but finish the work assigned.

DISCIPLINE AND PUNISHMENT

We covered the overarching why of Timothy's mission: love, based on the hope Jesus Christ provided in His death that believers take on these noble tasks because they have placed faith and confidence in God. However, a general view of love is misguided from God's perspective. The writer of Hebrews set the record straight, "The Lord disciplines the one He loves and chastises every son whom He receives" (*ESV*, 2001/2016, Hebrews 12:6). Scorgie et al. (2011) provided clarity by summarizing God's work in discipline by describing it as circumstances God allows or initiates to draw people to Himself to become more like Himself. At the same time, the circumstances may be painful, unpleasant, and delivered in a firm, direct manner, but discipline differs from punishment. Again, Scorgie et al. (2011) differentiated between the two by emphasizing punishment, which consists of penalties inflicted on an offender that may or may not lead to that person's reformation. The writer of Hebrews was confirming David's conclusions about the benefits of God's afflictions (Psalm 119:71, 75) while providing a sure foundation for John to build upon in Revelation 3:19. Discipline and punishment are tools of God's love administered to those He loves and accepts as His children.

Whether the circumstances warranted discipline or punishment, Paul urged Timothy to reject administering either in anger. When Paul experienced persecution, rejection, and desertion, he modeled for

Timothy the grace Jesus demonstrated on the cross when He asked His Father to forgive those perpetrating the heinous acts of crucifixion. Paul's prayer was that God would not charge them with any of the offenses they inflicted on him (2 Timothy 4:16). As the leader, Timothy was responsible for administering justice and correcting errors, but Paul insisted on carrying out the administration without discrimination (1 Timothy 5:21) or becoming quarrelsome (2 Timothy 2:24-25). Although they were undergoing slanderous persecution, Peter admonished the recipients of his letter to conduct their defense gently and respectfully (1 Peter 3:15). To say that Timothy was in a challenging position is a bit of an understatement. Still, Paul presented Timothy's situational circumstances not only for Timothy's benefit but for all who would come behind him – like you.

OBJECTIVES – LESSON TWO

TO DEMONSTRATE LOVE IN THE EXERCISE OF LEADERSHIP – 1 TIMOTHY 1:3-5

Timothy was the new guy on the block, yet Paul jumped right in and gave him commands that would put him at odds with the populace. The church in Ephesus had significant problems, primarily the false teachers. When Paul gave Timothy the bottom line up front, he told him to remain in Ephesus to silence the false teachers who were infecting the people with false doctrines and abuses of the law that were causing the people to act in a way that was displeasing to God (Fee, 1985). Heringer (2021) classified the false teaching as heterodoxy – teachings dependent on myths and genealogies resulting in arguments and broken relationships. Luke's record of the Ephesian church included Paul letting them know that some of the misleading instructions would come from within and deceive the people. Yet, the teaching of the false teachers attracted the people (Acts 20:30). This widespread perversion was what Timothy was up against. It would require him to do what was against his nature – speak boldly and authoritatively and command them to cease.

In the natural, commanding compliance would seem to be an act of the tyrannical; however, Paul framed it as loving. Earlier, we understood that these commands were acts of love designed to engender behavior modification by causing the people to turn from heterodoxy to orthodoxy – God's way of conducting oneself as contained in the gospel (Heringer, 2021). MacDonald (1990) surmised that the aim of love was not only orthodoxy but love coming from a pure heart, a clear conscience, and sincere faith. The love spoken of here encompasses loving God and loving one's associates in a way that is pure and void of hypocrisy (MacDonald, 1990). From a practical perspective, Evans and Holman (2019) noted, "The conscience is designed to serve as a megaphone directed at our souls to help us understand right from wrong and distinguish authentic Christian faith from false religion" (p. 1278). The motivations and modus operandi of the false teachers leaned towards deceitfulness, insincerity, and asceticism (1 Timothy 4:1-2), which tickled the ears (2 Timothy 4:3) because it sounded godly but lacked the power of true godliness (2 Timothy 3:5). Timothy had some difficult messages he had to deliver to some difficult people who were deceived and being deceived by demonic deputies (1 Timothy 4:1). Timothy would only persevere through the challenges and difficulties as he understood his why – love, flowing from a pure heart with a good conscience undergirded by sincere faith.

The same is true of you. God has given you the aspiration for leadership and will build into you the love needed to love His people enough to withstand their rejection and resistance. It would be best to do everything lovingly – even when verbal, physical, or spiritual challenges occur. You must remain consistent with the truths you have garnered from God's Word and godly advice. Willimon (2016) described the source of consistency as recognizing that God has summoned you to ministry, and Jesus repeatedly said that the only way to demonstrate love for Him was to obey His commands. You will have to love them as you verbally let them have it.

To Submit to the Accountability of Leadership – 1 Timothy 6:17-19

This objective contains two challenging words to grasp personally: submit and accountability. When looking at the first word about leadership, Hebrews 13:17 succinctly described the expectations when leadership communicated an objective, "Obey your leaders and submit to them." Evans and Holman (2019) added a limiting factor to this obedience and submission in that the direction provided by the leader must be in keeping with God's Word. When Strong (2009) defined submission, he explained it as yielding to authority as an act of the will where the person intentionally places themselves under another person's direction. The reasons for obeying and submitting include acknowledging the responsibility of leadership (to oversee) and then our second term, accountability. Leaders must give an account before God of their stewarding of the flock. Accountability is the language of stewardship because the steward must answer to someone for the choices, decisions, and actions of those for whom they are responsible (Scorgie et al., 2011). Paul emphasized Timothy's accountability to God for proclaiming the truths of God's Word and the responsibility of the people to respond humbly in obedience.

Submission and accountability are the fruit of humility. Timothy received a directive from Paul to ensure he planted the seed of humility in the hearts of the wealthy Ephesians to understand that their wealth was not their own and that God expected that they would willingly share with those in need (MacDonald, 1990). Timothy was to stress their connectedness to those of lesser means as an indication of their oneness in Christ. Submission and humility also provide a picture of our mutual accountability. As Engstrom (1978) suggested, everyone should have three types of accountability partners: 1) Timothy – someone you can pour into; 2) Barnabas – someone who can encourage you amid challenging circumstances as you interact with challenging people; and a peer group with whom you share accountability. You also need a Paul to disciple you and say, “Follow me as I follow Christ.”

Understanding how people should carry themselves is crucial, but it is equally important that you teach them the lessons and truths of our referenced passage. Earthly riches are an unsure source (Matthew 6:19); conversely, the blessings of God bring no sorrow (Proverbs 10:22). Not to mention, God has already provided you with everything you need for life and godliness (2 Peter 1:3). Your love of God combined with your sincere aspiration to serve must motivate you to give the commands to the people God has assigned to your care so that they can submit to you as you guide them according to God’s Word. Paul commanded Timothy; Timothy commanded the people; the people were to obey and submit to God’s will for their lives as Timothy told them, and you will say it to them lovingly and humbly.

TO ELIMINATE EVIL PRACTICES AND ESTABLISH GODLY PATTERNS – 2 TIMOTHY 2:14-15

This charge to Timothy is in Paul’s second letter to Timothy. The struggle with false teachers is still an issue Paul addresses in 2 Timothy 2:14 – 3:9. Our referenced verses are at the beginning of this section on false teaching and teachers and find Paul encouraging Timothy to persevere through the struggle and to remind the church of what they should be doing and what they should not be doing. When Evans and Holman (2019) addressed Paul’s instructions about false teaching, they noted that practicing and preaching about false doctrines was not enough because the Ephesians also needed the true meaning of Scripture to distinguish between the fake and the genuine.

Paul's impassioned plea to Timothy was for Timothy to passionately command the people not to become engaged in word games. There is something about being in God's presence that warrants solemnity. So, Paul told Timothy to remind the Ephesians that the command they were receiving had God as a witness. While MacDonald (1990) believed the charge was in keeping with verses 11-13, Evans and Holman (2019) focused on the charge relative to the inappropriate use of words. The FMIFC process incorporates both viewpoints. If the Ephesians were going to stand firm in their faith while false teachers and ungodly behavior became more commonplace (2 Timothy 3:1-5), they would need the foundation of who Jesus was, what He did, and what they could expect because of their following Christ, in time and eternity. Paul stressed to Timothy the absolute necessity of speaking the truths of the gospel into the people's hearing. Paul penned the words about hearing being the faith pathway (Romans 10:17) and the foolishness of preaching being the mechanism to inform people about God. Timothy must diligently preach the Word so that the people can delineate between truth and error. Then Paul pivots briefly to give Timothy a pointer about making his presentations more meaningful to his hearers. Mattke (1973) contended that the only way Paul, Timothy, or anyone else could make God's Word clear, understandable, relevant, and practical would be to study the Word diligently and conscientiously. When we looked at the objective from module two, lesson three, Practice Persistently the Principles of God's Word, we saw Paul's prescription for presentations for Timothy to practice using.

At some point, you must address foolish talking with your people. You cannot overlook it, so you must decide how to deal with it. Solomon noted two options for dealing with a fool – say nothing to the fool because in doing so you may become a fool or say something to the fool so that the fool does not become wise in his own eyes (Proverbs 26:4-5). This decision will call for spiritual discernment, so watch yourself. Consider having a friend to help keep you in check. Iron sharpening iron is a methodology to remain accountable. So, as you end this process, you need to begin addressing the accountability partners mentioned earlier. Each of you must be a Paul with someone in your life that you are discipling to provide the continuity of faithful witnesses mentioned in 2 Timothy 2:2 (Willimon, 2016). Find a godly person who is not impressed by your resume and is humble enough to respect your perspective. Young man, preach the Word as you prepare to have others follow you as you follow Christ.

CONCLUDING THOUGHT

While preparing for this academic process, I thought, "What lesson or sermon would be complete without a musical reminder, and who better to remind us than Charles Wesley?" While this song has its roots in Leviticus 8:35, I believe it is an appropriate reminder that if you aspire to the leadership of God's people, you have a calling that requires your life to display specific characteristics, especially as you endure the challenges of ministry as a youngster. You have "A Charge to Keep."

A Charge to Keep I Have

by Charles Wesley

1 A charge to keep I have,
a God to glorify,
a never-dying soul to save,
and fit it for the sky.

2 To serve the present age,
my calling to fulfill,

O may it all my pow'rs engage
to do my Master's will!

3 Arm me with watchful care
as in Thy sight to live,
and now Thy servant, Lord, prepare
a strict account to give!

4 Help me to watch and pray,
and still on Thee rely,
O let me not my trust betray,
but press to realms on high.

Since you have concluded this process, our learners and leaders have hopefully benefitted from the instruction narratives, pericope analysis, thought-provoking assessments, and increased awareness of your biblical vocabulary. The Follow Me as I Follow Christ process is a tool that will assist your fellowship in preparing your youth for positions of leadership while providing an instructional tool for those who would disciple them. There is a realization that the FMIFC is not a one-size-fits-all comprehensive solution, but it provides a catalytic jump start to succession management for your local church.

REFERENCES

Ammer, C. (2013). *The American Heritage dictionary of idioms: American English idiomatic expressions & phrases.* HMH.

Andelin, A. P. (1972). *Man of steel and velvet.* Pacific Press Santa Barbara.

Arp, W. (2012). Illumination: What is the Role of the Holy Spirit in Interpretation? *The Journal of Ministry & Theology, 16*(1), 50–86.

Bagby, D. G. (2017). Some assembly required. *Review & Expositor, 114*(2), 304–307.

Bard, T. R. (2018). Words, Meanings, and Consequences. *Journal of Pastoral Care & Counseling, 72*(3), 158-158.

Barker, K. L. (1989). Proverbs 23:"To Think" or "To Serve Food?". *Journal of the Ancient Near Eastern Society, 19*(1).

Barry, J. D., Mangum, D., Brown, D. R., Heiser, M. S., Custis, M., Ritzema, E., & Bomar, D. (2012). Faithlife study bible. *Bellingham, WA: Logos Bible Software.*

Bazerman, M. H., & Tenbrunsel, A. E. (2011). *Blind spots: Why we fail to do what's right and what to do about it.* Princeton University Press.

Beale, G. K. (Gregory K. (2023). The Greco-Roman Background to "Fighting the Good Fight" in the Pastoral Epistles and the Spiritual Life of the Christian. *Themelios, 48*(3), 541–551.

Belleville, L. L. (1989). A letter of apologetic self-commendation: 2 Cor 1:8-7:16. *Novum Testamentum, 31*(2), 142–163.

Blackaby, H. T., Blackaby, R., & King, C. V. (2022). *Experiencing God (2021 Edition): Knowing and Doing the Will of God.* B&H Publishing Group.

Bond, L. S. (2006). 1 Timothy 1:3-17. *Interpretation, 60*(3), 314–317.

Brown, S. (2015). What Is truth?: Jesus, Pilate, and the staging of the dialogue of the cross in John 18:28-19:16a. *The Catholic Biblical Quarterly, 77*(1), 69–86.

Bruce, F. F. (1980). *Paul, apostle of the heart set free.* Wm. B. Eerdmans Publishing.

Brueggemann, W. (1992). Pushing past into present. *The Christian Century, 109*(24), 741.

Bruehler, B. B. (2022). Expecting the Unexpected in Luke 7:1-10. *Tyndale Bulletin, 73,* 71–89

Bryant, R. A. (2004). Romans 12:1-8. *Interpretation, 58*(3), 287–290.

Burke, R. L. (2003). *Commentary on the General Directory for Catechesis.* Eternal Life.

Campbell, B. L. (1997). Rhetorical Design in 1 Timothy 4. *Bibliotheca Sacra, 154*(614), 189–204.

Catt, M. (2013, January 4). *The danger of mixing truth with error.* http://michaelcatt.com/2013/01/the-danger-of-mixing-truth-and-error/

Clark, R. R., Jr. (2006). Family management or involvement?: Paul's use of προίστημι in 1 Timothy 3 as a requirement for church leadership. *Stone-Campbell Journal, 9*(2), 243–252.

Clarke, A. D. (2007). A Pauline theology of church leadership. *A Pauline Theology of Church Leadership*, 1-220.

Cole, V. B. (2005). The message and messenger of the gospel. *Evangelical Review of Theology, 29*(2), 178–184

Covey, S. R. (2020). *The 7 habits of highly effective people.* Simon & Schuster.

Culpepper, R. A. (1986). The power of words and the tests of two wisdoms: James 3. *Review & Expositor, 83*(3), 405–417.

Dingeldein, L. B. (2013). "ότι πνευματκῶς ανακρίνεραι": examining translations of 1 Corinthians 2:14. *Novum Testamentum, 55*(1), 31–44.

Dionson, H. (2015). 1 Timothy 4:6-16: towards a theology of encouragement. *Asian Journal of Pentecostal Studies, 18*(2), 7–21.

Dodd, C. H. (1944). *The apostolic preaching and its developments* (p. 47). London: Hodder & Stoughton.

Donahue, J. R. (2002). The Word. *America, 187*(13), 31.

Dowd, S. (2015). Luke 9:18-27: "daily" cross-bearing for Jesus' sake. *Review & Expositor, 112*(4), 618–623.

English standard version (2016). Crossway Bibles. (*originally published in 2001*).

Engstrom, T. W. (1978). *The making of a Christian leader.* Zondervan.

Evans, T., & Holman, C. B. (2019). *The Tony Evans Bible Commentary: Advancing God's Kingdom Agenda.* B&H Publishing Group.

Fee, G. D. (1985). Reflections on church order in the Pastoral Epistles, with further reflection on the hermeneutics of ad hoc documents. *Journal of the Evangelical Theological Society, 28*(2), 141–151.

Garland, D. E. (1986). Severe trials, good gifts, and pure religion: James 1. *Review & Expositor, 83*(3), 383–394.

Glasscock, E. (1987). The biblical concept of elder. *Bibliotheca Sacra, 144*(573), 66–78.

Gleason, R. C. (1997). Paul's Covenantal Contrasts in 2 Corinthians 3:1-11. *Bibliotheca Sacra, 154*(613), 61–79.

Gray, D. (2014). Succession planning 101. *Professional Safety, 59*(3), 35.

Gresham, J. (2006). The divine pedagogy as a model for online education. *Teaching Theology & Religion, 9*(1), 24-28.

Grudem, W. A. (2014). *Bible doctrine: Essential teachings of the Christian faith.* Zondervan Academic.

Hackman, M. Z., & Johnson, C. E. (2013). *Leadership: A communication perspective.* Waveland press.

Hays, C. M. (2009). Hating wealth and wives?: an examination of discipleship ethics in the third gospel. *Tyndale Bulletin, 60*(1), 47–68.

Henry, M. (2000). *Commentary on the Whole Bible Volume VI (Acts to Revelation).* CCEL.

Heringer, S. (2021). Beginning with the End: 1 Timothy 1:3–6 and Formative Theological Education. *Journal of Theological Interpretation, 15*(2), 365–378.

House, R., & Marg, W. H. (2011). Dictionary. com. *Keyword: Persistence.*

Hull, W. E. (1959). The man Timothy. *Review & Expositor, 56*(4), 355–366.

Idowu, D. O. (2017). A Charge to Maintain Christian Value in 2 Timothy 3:10-4:5 and Its Implications for a Changing Society. *Ogbomoso Journal of Theology, 22*(2), 88–100.

Ituma, E. A., Peters, P. E., Ngele, O. K., & Agbo, P. O. (2021). Nigerian youth, politics and the demand for τολμηρήηγεσία: A study on I Timothy 4: 11–12. *HTS Teologiese Studies/Theological Studies, 77*(4).

Jamieson, R., Fausset, A. R., & Brown, D. (1997). Commentary Critical and Explanatory on the Whole Bible. 1871. *Logos Software.*

Jensen, E. S. (2021). How Did Jesus Do It? *The Way*, *60*(3), 63–64.

Kleinig, J. W. (2017). Paul's antidote for pastoral timidity in 2 Timothy 1:6-14. *Logia*, *26*(2), 7–10.

Kouzes, J. M., & Posner, B. Z. (2017). *The leadership challenge: How to make extraordinary things happen in organizations.* John Wiley & Sons.

Kuepfer, T. (2009). "I saw the light": the significance of the apostle Paul's conversion testimony. *Vision (Winnipeg, Man.)*, *10*(2), 13–19.

Lambrecht, J. (2001). The fool's speech and its context: Paul's particular way of arguing in 2 Cor 10-13. *Biblica*, *82*(3), 305–324.

Lambrecht, J. (2013). 1 Corinthians 2:14: a response to Laura B Dingeldein. *Novum Testamentum*, *55*(4), 367–370.

Lawson, S. J. (2002). The passion of biblical preaching: an expository study of 1 Timothy 4:13-16. *Bibliotheca Sacra*, *159*(633), 79–95.

Lim, T. H. (1987). "Not in persuasive words of wisdom, but in the demonstration of the spirit and power." *Novum Testamentum*, *29*(2), 137–149.

MacDonald, W. (1990). *Believer's Bible commentary*. Thomas Nelson.

MacGorman, J. W. (Jack W. (1986). An exposition of James 3. *Southwestern Journal of Theology*, *29*(1), 31–36.

Makins, M., & Isaacs, A. (1991). *Collins English dictionary* (3rd ed). HarperCollins Publishers.

Marzahn, P. (2021). *Church Planting Pastors: Identifying, Assessing, and Recruiting Potential Church Planting Leadership*. Asbury Theological Seminary.

Mattke, R. A. (1973). Integration of truth in John Wesley. *Wesleyan Theological Journal, 8*, 3–13.

Maxwell, J. C. (2001). *Developing the leader within you workbook.* HarperChristian Resources.

Mayhue, R. L. (2011). Authentic spiritual leadership. *The Master's Seminary Journal, 22*(2), 213–224.

Mayes, B. T. G. (2019). The Useful Applications of Scripture in Lutheran Orthodoxy: An Aid to Contemporary Preaching and Exegesis. *Concordia Theological Quarterly, 83*(1–2), 111–135.

McKenzie, A. M. (2006). 2 Timothy 1:3-7. *Interpretation, 60*(3), 318–320.

Merkle, B. L. (2014). Are the qualifications for elders or overseers negotiable? *Bibliotheca Sacra, 171*(682), 172–188.

Moessner, D. P. (1986). "The Christ must suffer": new light on the Jesus - Peter, Stephen, Paul parallels in Luke-Acts. *Novum Testamentum, 28*(3), 220–256.

Morgan, R. (1987). Faith, hope and love abide. *Churchman, 101*(2), 128–139.

Moşoiu, N. (2019). 'All who desire to live a godly life in Christ Jesus will be persecuted' (2 Tm 3:12): An Eastern Orthodox perspective on persecutions and martyrdom. *HTS Theological Studies, 75*(4), 1–11.

New International Version Bible. (1984) (Original work published in 1978)

Northouse, P. G. (2019). *Leadership: Theory and practice.* Sage publications.

Paskah Parlaungan Purba, Christian Johan Lasut, Wahyuni, S., & Lestari, A. (2022). Explanation and Confirmation of Education based on 2 Timothy 1:1-18 among Christian Religious Education Teachers in Batam City. *Pharos Journal of Theology, 103*(2), 1–18.

Perkins, P. (2020). Tongue on Fire: Ethics of Speech in James. *Interpretation, 74*(4), 363–373.

Pojman, L. P. (1995). *Ethical theory: classical and contemporary readings* (2nd ed.). Wadsworth Pub. Co.

Porter, C. L. (1987). "Wise as serpents, innocent as doves" how shall we live. *Encounter, 48*(1), 15–26.

Punt, J. (2013). Politics of genealogies in the New Testament. *Neotestamentica, 47*(2), 373–398.

Purba, P. P., Lasut, C. J., & Lestari, A. (2022). Explanation and Confirmation of Education based on 2 Timothy 1: 1-18 among Christian Religious Education Teachers in Batam City. *Pharos Journal of Theology, 103*(2).

Rothwell, W. (2010). *Effective succession planning: Ensuring leadership continuity and building talent from within*. Amacom.

Rowe, A. (1999). Preaching and teaching. *Evangel*, 48-52.

Schein, E. H. (2010). *Organizational culture and leadership* (Vol. 2). John Wiley & Sons.

Scholer, J. M. (2016). 1 Corinthians 15:1–11. *Interpretation, 70*(4), 475–477.

Scorgie, G. G., Chan, S., Smith, G. T., & Smith III, J. D. (Eds.). (2011). *Dictionary of Christian spirituality*. Zondervan Academic.

Scott, J. W. (2015). The misunderstood mustard seed: Matt 17:20b; Luke 17:6. *Trinity Journal, 36*(1), 25–48.

Searle, J. T. (2009). Is the Sermon on the Mount too unrealistic to serve as a resource for Christian discipleship and spiritual formation? *Journal of European Baptist Studies, 9*(2), 38–50.

Stevens, D. C. (1985). Apt to teach: preparation for ministry in a silicon society. *Christian Education Journal, 6*(1), 5–18.

Strauch, A. (2009). *Biblical Eldership*. Emmaus Correspondence School.

Strong, J. (2009). *Strong's exhaustive concordance of the Bible*. Hendrickson Publishers.

Sylva, D. D. (1987). The cryptic clause en tois tou patros mou dei einai me in Lk 2:49b. *Journal of New Testament Science and the Knowledge of the Older Church, 78*(1–2), 132–140.

Temple, P. J. (1939). "House or business" in Luke 2:49? *The Catholic Biblical Quarterly, 1*(4), 342–352.

Thomas, R. L., & Köstenberger, A. J. (2017). *1 and 2 Thessalonians, 1 and 2 Timothy, Titus*. Zondervan Academic.

Thornton, D. T. (2015). Satan as adversary and ally in the process of ecclesial discipline: the use of the prologue to Job in 1 Corinthians 5:5 and 1 Timothy 1:20. *Tyndale Bulletin, 66*(1), 137–151.

Unger, M. F. (2009). *The new Unger's Bible dictionary*. Moody Publishers.

Van Neste, R. (2022). Portrait of a Faithful, Approved Workman: An Exhortation to Seminarians-2 Timothy 2:14-26. *Criswell Theological Review, 20*(1), 107–118.

Veiss, S. D. (2018). Follower development: Paul's charge to Timothy. *Journal of Biblical Perspectives in Leadership, 8*(1), 150-167.

Verbrugge, V. D. (1980). Delivered over to Satan. *Reformed Journal, 30*(6), 17–19.

Vine, W. E., & Unger, M. (1996). *Vine's complete expository dictionary of Old and New Testament words: with topical index*. Thomas Nelson.

Walker, P. (2012). Revisiting the Pastoral Epistles -- Part I. *European Journal of Theology, 21*(1), 4–16.

Ward, R. F. (1990). 2 Corinthians 10:7-12. *Review & Expositor, 87*(4), 605–609.

Whittington, J. L., Pitts, T. M., Kageler, W. V., & Goodwin, V. L. (2005). Legacy leadership: The leadership wisdom of the Apostle Paul. *The Leadership Quarterly, 16*(5), 749-770.

Williams, A. M., & Hodges, N. J. (2005). Practice, instruction and skill acquisition in soccer: Challenging tradition. *Journal of Sports Sciences, 23*(6), 637-650.

Willimon, W. H. (2016). *Pastor: The theology and practice of ordained ministry.* Abingdon Press.

Willis, T. M. (1994). "Obey Your Leaders": Hebrews 13 and Leadership in the Church. *Restoration Quarterly, 36*(4), 316–326.

Wooden, J., & Jamison, Steve. (2005). *Wooden on leadership* (First edition.). McGraw-Hill.

Zaccaro, S. J., Mumford, M. D., Connelly, M. S., Marks, M. A., & Gilbert, J. A. (2000). Assessment of leader problem-solving capabilities. *The Leadership Quarterly, 11*(1), 37-64.

Ziglar, T. (2003). When words get in the way of true religion. *Review & Expositor, 100*(2), 269–277.

Zorn, R. O. (1991). "Preach the Word." *Mid-America Journal of Theology, 7*(1), 17–32.

Workbook Exercises for Leader Reflection and Refreshing and Learner Responsibility

Workbook Exercises for Module One: The Call of Leadership

Workbook Exercises for Module One, Lesson One: Establishing the Relationship

Scriptural Reflections

Passage for reflection: 1 Timothy 1:1

• What message was Paul conveying to Timothy in this passage?	
• What do you think Timothy's understanding of the passage was?	
• What are your takeaways for personal, relevant application?	

Passage for reflection: 1 Timothy 1:6-7

• What message was Paul conveying to Timothy in this passage?	
• What do you think Timothy's understanding of the passage was?	
• What are your takeaways for personal, relevant application?	

Passages for reflection: 1 Timothy 1:12-14

• What message was Paul conveying to Timothy in this passage?	
• What do you think Timothy's understanding of the passage was?	
• What are your takeaways for personal, relevant application?	

Passages for reflection: 1 Timothy 2:7

• What message was Paul conveying to Timothy in this passage?	
• What do you think Timothy's understanding of the passage was?	
• What are your takeaways for personal, relevant application?	

Passages for reflection: 1 Timothy 4:14

• What message was Paul conveying to Timothy in this passage?	
• What do you think Timothy's understanding of the passage was?	
• What are your takeaways for personal, relevant application?	

Passages for reflection: 1 Timothy 5:22

• What message was Paul conveying to Timothy in this passage?	
• What do you think Timothy's understanding of the passage was?	
• What are your takeaways for personal, relevant application?	

Passages for reflection: 2 Timothy 1:1

• What message was Paul conveying to Timothy in this passage?	
• What do you think Timothy's understanding of the passage was?	
• What are your takeaways for personal, relevant application?	

Passages for reflection: 2 Timothy 1:6

• What message was Paul conveying to Timothy in this passage?	
• What do you think Timothy's understanding of the passage was?	
• What are your takeaways for personal, relevant application?	

Passages for reflection: 2 Timothy 1:8-14

• What message was Paul conveying to Timothy in this passage?	
• What do you think Timothy's understanding of the passage was?	
• What are your takeaways for personal, relevant application?	

Passages for reflection: 2 Timothy 2:2

• What message was Paul conveying to Timothy in this passage?	
• What do you think Timothy's understanding of the passage was?	
• What are your takeaways for personal, relevant application?	

Passages for reflection: 2 Timothy 3:10-17

• What message was Paul conveying to Timothy in this passage?	
• What do you think Timothy's understanding of the passage was?	
• What are your takeaways for personal, relevant application?	

Assessment: Reflective Exercise – Module One, Lesson One

• What led you to believe God called you to leadership?	
• How would you encourage youth to step up to leadership challenges?	
• What characteristics would you look for in a leader?	

Vocabulary and Key Words – Module One, Lesson One

• Service: 1 Tim. 1:12	
• Teacher: 1 Tim. 2:7, 2 Tim. 1:11	
• Overseer: 1 Tim. 3:1	
• Calling: 2 Tim. 1:9	
• Reproof: 2 Tim. 3:16	
• Correction: 2 Tim. 3:16	
• Training in Righteousness: 2 Tim. 3:16	

Workbook Exercises for Module One, Lesson Two: Determining the Certainty of Calling

Scriptural Reflections

Passage for reflection: 1 Timothy 1:1

• What message was Paul conveying to Timothy in this passage?	
• What do you think Timothy's understanding of the passage was?	
• What are your takeaways for personal, relevant application?	

Passage for reflection: 1 Timothy 2:7

• What message was Paul conveying to Timothy in this passage?	
• What do you think Timothy's understanding of the passage was?	
• What are your takeaways for personal, relevant application?	

Passages for reflection: 2 Timothy 1:1

• What message was Paul conveying to Timothy in this passage?	
• What do you think Timothy's understanding of the passage was?	
• What are your takeaways for personal, relevant application?	

Passages for reflection: 2 Timothy 1:11

• What message was Paul conveying to Timothy in this passage?	
• What do you think Timothy's understanding of the passage was?	
• What are your takeaways for personal, relevant application?	

Assessment: Reflective Exercise – Module One, Lesson Two

• Spend some time remembering the early days of your calling. How did people respond to your leadership?	
• What were your areas of concern, and how did you overcome them? How are you working on overcoming them?	
• What was the impact of the person/people guiding you throughout the process?	

Vocabulary and Key Words – Module One, Lesson Two

• Command: 1 Tim. 1:1	
• Apostle: 1 Tim. 1:1, 2:7, 2 Tim. 1:1, 11	
• Appointed: 1 Tim. 2:7, 2 Tim. 1:11	

Workbook Exercises for Module One, Lesson Three: Identifying the Category of Calling

Scriptural Reflections

Passage for reflection: 1 Timothy 2:7

• What message was Paul conveying to Timothy in this passage?	
• What do you think Timothy's understanding of the passage was?	
• What are your takeaways for personal, relevant application?	

Passage for reflection: 1 Timothy 3:1

• What message was Paul conveying to Timothy in this passage?	
• What do you think Timothy's understanding of the passage was?	
• What are your takeaways for personal, relevant application?	

Passages for reflection: 1 Timothy 3:8

• What message was Paul conveying to Timothy in this passage?	
• What do you think Timothy's understanding of the passage was?	
• What are your takeaways for personal, relevant application?	

Passages for reflection: 2 Timothy 1:6

• What message was Paul conveying to Timothy in this passage?	
• What do you think Timothy's understanding of the passage was?	
• What are your takeaways for personal, relevant application?	

Passages for reflection: 2 Timothy 1:11

• What message was Paul conveying to Timothy in this passage?	
• What do you think Timothy's understanding of the passage was?	
• What are your takeaways for personal, relevant application?	

Assessment: Reflective Exercise – Module One, Lesson Three

• What was your idea of an "elder" when you were growing up? Over the years, how has the concept developed?	
• What do you believe are your areas of Spiritual gifting? How has God revealed that to you?	
• How have you interacted with Deacons before? What do you believe the relationship should be between the elders and deacons?	

Vocabulary and Key Words – Module One, Lesson Three

• Deacon: 1 Tim. 3:8	
• Gift: 1 Tim. 4:14, 2 Tim. 1:6	
• Good Work: 2 Tim. 3:17	

Workbook Exercises for Module Two: The Character of Leadership

Workbook Exercises for Module Two, Lesson One: Defining Character

Scriptural Reflections

Passage for reflection: 1 Timothy 1:12

• What message was Paul conveying to Timothy in this passage?	
• What do you think Timothy's understanding of the passage was?	
• What are your takeaways for personal, relevant application?	

Passage for reflection: 1 Timothy 6:8

• What message was Paul conveying to Timothy in this passage?	
• What do you think Timothy's understanding of the passage was?	
• What are your takeaways for personal, relevant application?	

Passages for reflection: 1 Timothy 6:11

• What message was Paul conveying to Timothy in this passage?	
• What do you think Timothy's understanding of the passage was?	
• What are your takeaways for personal, relevant application?	

Passages for reflection: 2 Timothy 1:7

• What message was Paul conveying to Timothy in this passage?	
• What do you think Timothy's understanding of the passage was?	
• What are your takeaways for personal, relevant application?	

Passages for reflection: 2 Timothy 1:14

• What message was Paul conveying to Timothy in this passage?	
• What do you think Timothy's understanding of the passage was?	
• What are your takeaways for personal, relevant application?	

Passages for reflection: 2 Timothy 2:2

• What message was Paul conveying to Timothy in this passage?	
• What do you think Timothy's understanding of the passage was?	
• What are your takeaways for personal, relevant application?	

Passages for reflection: 2 Timothy 2:10

• What message was Paul conveying to Timothy in this passage?	
• What do you think Timothy's understanding of the passage was?	
• What are your takeaways for personal, relevant application?	

Passages for reflection: 2 Timothy 3:14

• What message was Paul conveying to Timothy in this passage?	
• What do you think Timothy's understanding of the passage was?	
• What are your takeaways for personal, relevant application?	

Assessment: Reflective Exercise – Module Two, Lesson One

• How does your reputation compare to your character?	
• What are you doing to encourage others to develop Christlike character?	
• If you were Paul, how would Timothy be able to imitate you? Where would they go? What would they see? What would you ask Timothy to do?	

Vocabulary and Key Words – Module Two, Lesson One

• Faithful: 1 Tim. 1:12, 3:11, 2 Tim. 2:2	
• Content: 1 Tim. 6:8	
• Righteousness: 1 Tim. 6:11, 2 Tim. 2:22, 3:16, 4:8	
• Godliness: 1 Tim. 3:16, 4:7-8, 6: 3, 5-6, 11, 2 Tim. 3:5	
• Steadfastness: 1 Tim. 6:11, 2 Tim. 3:10	
• Gentleness: 1 Tim. 6:11, 2 Tim. 2:25	
• Love: 1 Tim. 1:5, 4:12, 6:11, 2 Tim. 1:7, 13, 2:22, 3:10	
• Self-control: 2 Tim. 1:7	

Workbook Exercises for Module Two, Lesson Two: Assessing the Content of My Character

Scriptural Reflections

Passage for reflection: 1 Timothy 1:12

• What message was Paul conveying to Timothy in this passage?	
• What do you think Timothy's understanding of the passage was?	
• What are your takeaways for personal, relevant application?	

Passage for reflection: 1 Timothy 1:19-20

• What message was Paul conveying to Timothy in this passage?	
• What do you think Timothy's understanding of the passage was?	
• What are your takeaways for personal, relevant application?	

Passages for reflection: 1 Timothy 2:7

• What message was Paul conveying to Timothy in this passage?	
• What do you think Timothy's understanding of the passage was?	
• What are your takeaways for personal, relevant application?	

Passages for reflection: 1 Timothy 3:7

• What message was Paul conveying to Timothy in this passage?	
• What do you think Timothy's understanding of the passage was?	
• What are your takeaways for personal, relevant application?	

Passages for reflection: 1 Timothy 5:1-2

• What message was Paul conveying to Timothy in this passage?	
• What do you think Timothy's understanding of the passage was?	
• What are your takeaways for personal, relevant application?	

Passages for reflection: 1 Timothy 6:8

• What message was Paul conveying to Timothy in this passage?	
• What do you think Timothy's understanding of the passage was?	
• What are your takeaways for personal, relevant application?	

Passages for reflection: 1 Timothy 6:11

• What message was Paul conveying to Timothy in this passage?	
• What do you think Timothy's understanding of the passage was?	
• What are your takeaways for personal, relevant application?	

Passages for reflection: 1 Timothy 6:21

• What message was Paul conveying to Timothy in this passage?	
• What do you think Timothy's understanding of the passage was?	
• What are your takeaways for personal, relevant application?	

Passage for reflection: 2 Timothy 1:7

• What message was Paul conveying to Timothy in this passage?	
• What do you think Timothy's understanding of the passage was?	
• What are your takeaways for personal, relevant application?	

Passage for reflection: 2 Timothy 1:15

• What message was Paul conveying to Timothy in this passage?	
• What do you think Timothy's understanding of the passage was?	
• What are your takeaways for personal, relevant application?	

Passages for reflection: 2 Timothy 2:2

• What message was Paul conveying to Timothy in this passage?	
• What do you think Timothy's understanding of the passage was?	
• What are your takeaways for personal, relevant application?	

Passages for reflection: 2 Timothy 2:10

• What message was Paul conveying to Timothy in this passage?	
• What do you think Timothy's understanding of the passage was?	
• What are your takeaways for personal, relevant application?	

Passages for reflection: 2 Timothy 2:17

• What message was Paul conveying to Timothy in this passage?	
• What do you think Timothy's understanding of the passage was?	
• What are your takeaways for personal, relevant application?	

Passages for reflection: 2 Timothy 3:12

• What message was Paul conveying to Timothy in this passage?	
• What do you think Timothy's understanding of the passage was?	
• What are your takeaways for personal, relevant application?	

Passages for reflection: 2 Timothy 3:15-17

• What message was Paul conveying to Timothy in this passage?	
• What do you think Timothy's understanding of the passage was?	
• What are your takeaways for personal, relevant application?	

Passages for reflection: 2 Timothy 4:10

• What message was Paul conveying to Timothy in this passage?	
• What do you think Timothy's understanding of the passage was?	
• What are your takeaways for personal, relevant application?	

Assessment: Reflective Exercise – Module Two, Lesson Two

• What is an example of an emotion-driven decision? What would you have done differently had the decision been character-driven?	
• What would give you the confidence/boldness to tell followers to imitate you?	
• How much time have you spent counting the cost of discipleship? (Luke14:33)	

Vocabulary and Key Words – Module Two, Lesson Two

• Reputation: 1 Tim. 5:10	
• Endurance: 2 Tim. 2:10	

Workbook Exercises for
Module Two, Lesson Three: Developing the Godly Quality of My Character

Scriptural Reflections

Passage for reflection: 1 Timothy 1:12

• What message was Paul conveying to Timothy in this passage?	
• What do you think Timothy's understanding of the passage was?	
• What are your takeaways for personal, relevant application?	

Passage for reflection: 1 Timothy 4:6

• What message was Paul conveying to Timothy in this passage?	
• What do you think Timothy's understanding of the passage was?	
• What are your takeaways for personal, relevant application?	

Passages for reflection: 1 Timothy 5:1-2

• What message was Paul conveying to Timothy in this passage?	
• What do you think Timothy's understanding of the passage was?	
• What are your takeaways for personal, relevant application?	

Passages for reflection: 1 Timothy 6:8

• What message was Paul conveying to Timothy in this passage?	
• What do you think Timothy's understanding of the passage was?	
• What are your takeaways for personal, relevant application?	

Passages for reflection: 1 Timothy 6:11

• What message was Paul conveying to Timothy in this passage?	
• What do you think Timothy's understanding of the passage was?	
• What are your takeaways for personal, relevant application?	

Passages for reflection: 2 Timothy 1:4

• What message was Paul conveying to Timothy in this passage?	
• What do you think Timothy's understanding of the passage was?	
• What are your takeaways for personal, relevant application?	

Passages for reflection: 2 Timothy 1:7

• What message was Paul conveying to Timothy in this passage?	
• What do you think Timothy's understanding of the passage was?	
• What are your takeaways for personal, relevant application?	

Passages for reflection: 2 Timothy 2:2

• What message was Paul conveying to Timothy in this passage?	
• What do you think Timothy's understanding of the passage was?	
• What are your takeaways for personal, relevant application?	

Passage for reflection: 2 Timothy 2:10

• What message was Paul conveying to Timothy in this passage?	
• What do you think Timothy's understanding of the passage was?	
• What are your takeaways for personal, relevant application?	

Passage for reflection: 2 Timothy 2:25

• What message was Paul conveying to Timothy in this passage?	
• What do you think Timothy's understanding of the passage was?	
• What are your takeaways for personal, relevant application?	

Passages for reflection: 2 Timothy 3:12

• What message was Paul conveying to Timothy in this passage?	
• What do you think Timothy's understanding of the passage was?	
• What are your takeaways for personal, relevant application?	

Passages for reflection: 2 Timothy 4:7

• What message was Paul conveying to Timothy in this passage?	
• What do you think Timothy's understanding of the passage was?	
• What are your takeaways for personal, relevant application?	

Passages for reflection: 2 Timothy 4:11

• What message was Paul conveying to Timothy in this passage?	
• What do you think Timothy's understanding of the passage was?	
• What are your takeaways for personal, relevant application?	

Passages for reflection: 2 Timothy 4:16

• What message was Paul conveying to Timothy in this passage?	
• What do you think Timothy's understanding of the passage was?	
• What are your takeaways for personal, relevant application?	

Assessment: Reflective Exercise – Module Two, Lesson Three

• For which Christlike attribute would you like to be known? Why?	
• What role does a godly character have in a leader's effectiveness?	
• Complete the Values in Action (VIA) Character Strength Survey. How can this tool impact your leadership team? What did it tell you about yourself? https://www.viacharacter.org/survey/account/Register	

Vocabulary and Key Words – Module Two, Lesson Three

• Servant: 1 Tim. 4:6	
• Joy: 2 Tim. 1:4	
• Teacher: 1 Tim. 2:7; 2 Tim. 1:11	
• Forgiveness: 2 Tim. 4:16	

Workbook Exercises for Module Three: The Challenges of Leadership

Workbook Exercises for Module Three, Lesson One: Why Leaders Face Challenges

Scriptural Reflections

Passage for reflection: 1 Timothy 1:3-11

• What message was Paul conveying to Timothy in this passage?	
• What do you think Timothy's understanding of the passage was?	
• What are your takeaways for personal, relevant application?	

Passage for reflection: 1 Timothy 2:8

• What message was Paul conveying to Timothy in this passage?	
• What do you think Timothy's understanding of the passage was?	
• What are your takeaways for personal, relevant application?	

Passages for reflection: 1 Timothy 4:1-5

• What message was Paul conveying to Timothy in this passage?	
• What do you think Timothy's understanding of the passage was?	
• What are your takeaways for personal, relevant application?	

Passages for reflection: 1 Timothy 4:12

• What message was Paul conveying to Timothy in this passage?	
• What do you think Timothy's understanding of the passage was?	
• What are your takeaways for personal, relevant application?	

Passages for reflection: 2 Timothy 3:1-9

• What message was Paul conveying to Timothy in this passage?	
• What do you think Timothy's understanding of the passage was?	
• What are your takeaways for personal, relevant application?	

Passages for reflection: 2 Timothy 4:9-18

• What message was Paul conveying to Timothy in this passage?	
• What do you think Timothy's understanding of the passage was?	
• What are your takeaways for personal, relevant application?	

Assessment: Reflective Exercise – Module Three, Lesson One

• How have you responded to opposition in the past? How has opposition impacted your leadership philosophy?	
• Think of an instance when you have faced internal opposition. What was the background incident? How did the people involved benefit?	
• How do you feel about Paul's statement to Timothy in 2 Timothy 3:12 – "All who desire to live a godly life in Christ Jesus will be persecuted?"	

Vocabulary and Key Words – Module Three, Lesson One

• Abstinence: 1 Tim. 4:3	
• Purity: 1 Tim. 4:12	
• Stewardship: 1 Tim. 1:4	
• Unappeasable: 2 Tim. 3:3	

Workbook Exercises for Module Three, Lesson Two: Challenges – Who and What

Scriptural Reflections

Passage for reflection: 1 Timothy 1:3-11

• What message was Paul conveying to Timothy in this passage?	
• What do you think Timothy's understanding of the passage was?	
• What are your takeaways for personal, relevant application?	

Passage for reflection: 1 Timothy 2:9-15

• What message was Paul conveying to Timothy in this passage?	
• What do you think Timothy's understanding of the passage was?	
• What are your takeaways for personal, relevant application?	

Passages for reflection: 1 Timothy 4:1-5

• What message was Paul conveying to Timothy in this passage?	
• What do you think Timothy's understanding of the passage was?	
• What are your takeaways for personal, relevant application?	

Passages for reflection: 1 Timothy 4:12

• What message was Paul conveying to Timothy in this passage?	
• What do you think Timothy's understanding of the passage was?	
• What are your takeaways for personal, relevant application?	

Passages for reflection: 1 Timothy 6:1-10

• What message was Paul conveying to Timothy in this passage?	
• What do you think Timothy's understanding of the passage was?	
• What are your takeaways for personal, relevant application?	

Passages for reflection: 2 Timothy 3:1-9

• What message was Paul conveying to Timothy in this passage?	
• What do you think Timothy's understanding of the passage was?	
• What are your takeaways for personal, relevant application?	

Assessment: Reflective Exercise – Module Three, Lesson Two

• Which do you consider the most challenging, people or situations? Why?	
• How has your background, i.e., where you were born, raised, educated, influenced your followers? Or, what impact do you believe it will have?	
• What challenges have you faced before? Based on your study of the FMIFC process, what, if anything, would you do differently?	

Vocabulary and Key Words – Module Three, Lesson Two

• **Speculation:** 1 Tim. 1:4	
• **Dissension:** 1 Tim. 6:4	
• **Depraved:** 1 Tim. 6:5	

Workbook Exercises for Module Three, Lesson Three: Overcoming Complexities of Leadership

Scriptural Reflections

Passage for reflection: 1 Timothy 3:1-13

• What message was Paul conveying to Timothy in this passage?	
• What do you think Timothy's understanding of the passage was?	
• What are your takeaways for personal, relevant application?	

Passage for reflection: 1 Timothy 4:12-14

• What message was Paul conveying to Timothy in this passage?	
• What do you think Timothy's understanding of the passage was?	
• What are your takeaways for personal, relevant application?	

Passages for reflection: 1 Timothy 6:1-10

• What message was Paul conveying to Timothy in this passage?	
• What do you think Timothy's understanding of the passage was?	
• What are your takeaways for personal, relevant application?	

Passages for reflection: 1 Timothy 6:20

• What message was Paul conveying to Timothy in this passage?	
• What do you think Timothy's understanding of the passage was?	
• What are your takeaways for personal, relevant application?	

Passages for reflection: 2 Timothy 1:6

• What message was Paul conveying to Timothy in this passage?	
• What do you think Timothy's understanding of the passage was?	
• What are your takeaways for personal, relevant application?	

Passages for reflection: 2 Timothy 1:13-14

• What message was Paul conveying to Timothy in this passage?	
• What do you think Timothy's understanding of the passage was?	
• What are your takeaways for personal, relevant application?	

Passages for reflection: 2 Timothy 2:1-7

• What message was Paul conveying to Timothy in this passage?	
• What do you think Timothy's understanding of the passage was?	
• What are your takeaways for personal, relevant application?	

Passages for reflection: 2 Timothy 3:14

• What message was Paul conveying to Timothy in this passage?	
• What do you think Timothy's understanding of the passage was?	
• What are your takeaways for personal, relevant application?	

Passages for reflection: 2 Timothy 4:5

• What message was Paul conveying to Timothy in this passage?	
• What do you think Timothy's understanding of the passage was?	
• What are your takeaways for personal, relevant application?	

Assessment: Reflective Exercise – Module Three, Lesson Three

• Other than the FMIFC process, who and what has prepared you for a ministry assignment? How?	
• How could the mentoring/preparation process have been improved?	
• What are you doing, or will you do, to prepare your successor for the challenges of leadership?	

Vocabulary and Key Words – Module Three, Lesson Three

• Doctrine: 1 Tim. 6:3	
• Bondservants: 1 Tim. 6:1	
• Content: 1 Tim. 6:6, 8	

Workbook Exercises for Module Four: The Charges to Leadership

Workbook Exercises for
Module Four, Lesson One: A Charge to Keep

Scriptural Reflections

Passage for reflection: 1 Timothy 1:5

• What message was Paul conveying to Timothy in this passage?	
• What do you think Timothy's understanding of the passage was?	
• What are your takeaways for personal, relevant application?	

Passage for reflection: 1 Timothy 1:17-19

• What message was Paul conveying to Timothy in this passage?	
• What do you think Timothy's understanding of the passage was?	
• What are your takeaways for personal, relevant application?	

Passages for reflection: 1 Timothy 5:18-22

• What message was Paul conveying to Timothy in this passage?	
• What do you think Timothy's understanding of the passage was?	
• What are your takeaways for personal, relevant application?	

Passages for reflection: 1 Timothy 6:12-14

• What message was Paul conveying to Timothy in this passage?	
• What do you think Timothy's understanding of the passage was?	
• What are your takeaways for personal, relevant application?	

Passages for reflection: 2 Timothy 4:1-2

• What message was Paul conveying to Timothy in this passage?	
• What do you think Timothy's understanding of the passage was?	
• What are your takeaways for personal, relevant application?	

Assessment: Reflective Exercise – Module Four, Lesson One

• Complete the Leadership Circle Profile at https://leadershipcircle.com/free-self-assessment/ . Based on your results, assess your leadership style.	
• When was an instance of someone you lead mistreating or disrespecting you? How did you handle it? After FMIFC, how would you handle it differently?	
• What do you do to resist focusing on anything other than the Word during your time of sermon preparation?	

Vocabulary and Key Words – Module Four, Lesson One

• Charge: 1 Tim. 1:3, 5, 18, 6:13, 17	
• Shipwreck: 1 Tim. 1:19	
• Charge: 1 Tim. 5:21, 2 Tim. 2:14, 4:1	
• Reprove: 2 Tim. 4:2	

Workbook Exercises for Module Four, Lesson Two: A Charge to Give

Scriptural Reflections

Passage for reflection: 1 Timothy 1:2-4

• What message was Paul conveying to Timothy in this passage?	
• What do you think Timothy's understanding of the passage was?	
• What are your takeaways for personal, relevant application?	

Passage for reflection: 1 Timothy 1:5

• What message was Paul conveying to Timothy in this passage?	
• What do you think Timothy's understanding of the passage was?	
• What are your takeaways for personal, relevant application?	

Passages for reflection: 1 Timothy 6:16-18

• What message was Paul conveying to Timothy in this passage?	
• What do you think Timothy's understanding of the passage was?	
• What are your takeaways for personal, relevant application?	

Passages for reflection: 2 Timothy 2:14

• What message was Paul conveying to Timothy in this passage?	
• What do you think Timothy's understanding of the passage was?	
• What are your takeaways for personal, relevant application?	

Assessment: Reflective Exercise – Module Four, Lesson Two

• To whom do you look to for human accountability? How did you develop a relationship with this person?	
• What do you consider to be the key(s) to disagreeing without becoming disagreeable and querying without becoming quarrelsome?	
• How have your views on discipline and punishment evolved with your spiritual maturation?	

Vocabulary and Key Words – Module Four, Lesson Two

• Speculations: 1 Tim. 1:4	
• Faith: 1 Tim. 1:5	
• Haughty: 1 Tim. 6:17	
• Quarrel: 2 Tim. 2:14	

Printed in the United States
by Baker & Taylor Publisher Services